Shark Weak

Overcoming the Weaknesses That Bite

Dr. Jeremy McGarity

To Janie, my partner in life and ministry, and to our kids, Riley, Aidan, and Levi—I am so thankful for you! I love you and couldn't do this without you.

And to our Skyline Church family—thank you for being a church where "No Perfect People Allowed" means we are all on this journey together, helping each other overcome the weaknesses that bite.

No matter where you are in your spiritual walk with Jesus Christ, Jeremy McGarity's *Shark Weak* lays out a playbook to bring you closer to the Prince of Peace. Jeremy examines things that hold a person back from being who God intended them to be. More importantly, he teaches you just how to do it.

Jayce Tingler, Manager, San Diego Padres, MLB

Sharks, be warned: you've been tagged! Jeremy has a masterful way of identifying predators, breaking down complex problems, and leading us to understandable solutions. Trust me, you'll find yourself inside the pages of this book. If you're looking for safer waters to swim in, read it more than once. Then read it again!

Tom Mercer, Lead Pastor, High Desert Church

A few years ago, we surveyed 1,000 people from every state, asking the question, "What one factor destroys hope, ruins relationships, and derails someone from having a great future?" When the surveys were done, we discovered this: the most important thing anyone can do to build a great future [is] play great defense! All of us have one thing in common right now—we are living in the craziest time in history and under more pressure than any previous generation. Jeremy McGarity's new book could not have arrived at a better time. It is a must-read. Why? Every person creates their future. This is a roadmap that will lead you to a future with far more joy than regrets.

Ray Johnston, Senior Pastor, Bayside Church, Granite Bay, CA

Jeremy McGarity delivers practical, biblical, and life-changing process in *Shark Weak* that will help you overcome the weaknesses that prevent you from becoming the person that God has designed you to be. It's surprisingly easy to drift from God, cave in to temptation, or become discouraged in life. Jeremy brings you, in a creative approach, solid answers to life's difficult challenges. Whether you are a new Christian or you've been walking with God for many years, this book will bring valuable insights that can change your life for the better!

Dan Reiland, Executive Pastor, 12Stone Church, Lawrenceville, GA

Jeremy has written a wonderful little book on the Christian life and the common struggles of Christ followers. The Christian life is a perilous journey rife with challenges—some from the outside, but mostly from within. Jeremy offers clear and thoughtful guidance for navigating this journey, including key biblical texts that speak to each specific challenge. May this resource help many as they seek to walk with God through this brief but challenging pilgrimage.

Brooks Buser, President, Radius International

CONTENTS

Overcoming Weakness 3

The Dangers of Drifting 7

Don't Let Worry Drag You Down 29

Identify the Bait 53

Don't Complain About the Water 73

Stop Biting Others 97

Don't Feed the Sharks! 119

Take the Bite Out of Your Words 141

It's Time to Swim 159

About the Author 161

Notes 164

INTRODUCTION

Overcoming Weakness

With care, he puts one foot in the legging of the wetsuit and pulls the tight rubber mesh up, over his knee. He puts his other foot in the other leg and stands. Wiggling, he yanks the suit over his thighs and swim trunks, belly, and chest, and twists like a ballerina to get his arms down the narrow sleeves. Then, *zip*—he's sealed in.

He grabs a mask and pulls it over his head. With help, he manages to get thirty-two pounds of oxygen tanks strapped to his back. Slipping his feet into flippers, he waddles like a duck toward the boat's edge. He settles his backside on the rail, oxygen flowing through the hose, and tips backward. Falling, falling, then *splash*—the cold envelopes him. He breathes as normally as he can as he adjusts to the depths around him.

With care, he quickly surveys his surroundings. Why? Because here be sharks. And, they are hungry.

Why dive into shark-infested water? Isn't it enough to dive into crushing depths? To venture so far from the surface that you need to depend on the limited air supply brought with you? To find your companions floating nearby, just as vulnerable as you are, breathing out of their hose?

Now, to this scenario, add carnivorous beasts that appear out of the darkness. They can grow to twenty feet, the same length as a London bus, or as tall as a giraffe. A great white shark can weigh 6,600 pounds—nearly the weight of two Ford Taurus cars. They have twenty to twenty-eight teeth on the top, and the same number on the bottom, which can grow as long as six-and-a-half inches. Measure from the tip of your finger up your arm and see how long a shark's tooth is.[1]

They can smell blood from a third of a mile away, and they'll swim toward the scent to feed.[2] Did you cut yourself when you entered the water? You might want to get out—fast.

But, what happens when you can't leave the water? What do you do when you live in a world where sharks exist all the time, circling, waiting to devour you at the first smell of blood?

You and I live in a world where sharks are our weakness—swimming around us, ready to lunge. Sometimes they nibble incessantly. And, we live in the water. How do we survive?

Yet we have a way out: God's Word. It tells us how to get out of the water—how to escape the gnawing, carnivorous beasts.

We are all looking to overcome the weaknesses that bite. I've written this book specifically to help you overcome weakness. No one particularly wants to be devoured by sharks, any more than they want to give in to weakness.

But, when they creep up on us, what do we do about them? How do we overcome them?

Before we proceed, let me define what I mean by the word *weakness*. A weakness is anything that keeps us from being who we were created to be—that is, conformed to the image of Christ (Romans 8:29). For example, when we drift away from the Lord—when we worry, when we complain or give in to anger or gossip—we are vulnerable to shark attacks. Temptation and lack of self-control are other weaknesses that keep us from being transformed.

This isn't pop psychology. This isn't scientific guesswork from flawed studies on how the brain works, or the latest fashion and diet to make you look better and trimmer, or feel good. This is where pain and suffering eat your soul—where issues meet us and we're crying for answers. The Scriptures provide the answers!

Every issue we deal with can be approached through the Word of God. The Bible gives us practical ways to handle things. Scripture isn't some theoretical model that sometimes works in our lives. It has every answer to every problem that has arisen since the beginning of time. "There is nothing new under the sun" (Ecclesiastes 1:9), so you can't come up with a problem the Bible knows nothing about.

As you journey through this book, I encourage you to get in the habit of asking, "What does God tell us to do?" Workbook sections after each chapter will help you discover and understand what to do about the problems you face, and will give you practical opportunities to apply the remedies from God's Word to your life.

You're swimming with sharks, and you're going to get bitten. Knowing that we need to get out of the water and *actually* getting out of the water are two different things. It's only when we get out of the water that we are safe from the shark bites.

Let's take a look at common weaknesses and discover what the Bible says about overcoming them.

CHAPTER ONE

The Dangers of Drifting

One of the Discovery Channel's most popular programs is Shark Week. If you watch Discovery during Shark Week, you'll see how sharks swim below the waves, lurking unseen except for the fin that juts out of the water. I'm talking specifically about great whites and the attacking sharks—the predators that are constantly looking for food, eager to sink their teeth into flesh.

Sharks hunt with a purpose. They'll drive straight into a pack of seals to try to separate one from the group, making the lone seal the perfect target.

The same is true with Satan. The enemy is a predator in your life. He's trying to divide and separate you from the pack—always trying to keep you from going to church, from participating in small group, from interacting with people who can encourage you. He is always, without rest, trying to divide you from the pack and conquer you. In short, he wants you to drift away.

On Drifting and Drifters: Separation

Sometimes, we let the waves carry us from shore. Or, the currents pull us from where we're going. For one reason or another, we drift away.

What do you do when you've drifted away from God? What about when you feel far away from your faith? How do you get close to God?

One of the main weaknesses that bites all of us is drifting away from our connection with God. This happens to everyone at some point. Instead of intentionally growing in our relationship, we just go with the flow, and before we know it, we don't feel as close to God as we once did. And, not only do we *feel* that, but we truly *aren't* close to Him.

Or, for some of you who are not yet believers, you have just been going with the flow of life. You've been drifting along, looking for the pleasures of life and running from things that make you sad.

Here's a question I ask myself and you must ask yourself as well: Has there ever been a time in your life when you felt closer to God than you do today?

If your answer is, "Yes, there was a time in my life when I felt closer to God," then let's learn how you can get back to feeling close to God again. If it's, "No, I'm as close to God as I've ever been," then what you're going to learn is how to get (and stay) in close relationship with God.

Note that in order to have a thriving relationship with Jesus Christ, you have to swim against the cultural current. Because the cultural current naturally pulls you away from faith and a relationship with Jesus Christ.

In one sense, we're all drifters. Sometimes we feel on fire for the Lord, and other times we feel distant. That's why, if you come to Skyline Church, where I preach, you will see a sign outside that says, "No perfect people allowed." No one lives a perfect faith journey. The goal in our journey is progress, not perfection.

What Do We Do If We're Separated from God?

Our relationship with Jesus Christ is, in so many ways, like any of our relationships. This is one of the keys to understanding how to stay close to God: for the relationship to work, it must be maintained. Relationships are always changing, morphing into new and sometimes interesting shapes. It's impossible for them to stay the same—people change. And, if people change, relationships change with them.

For those who are married, how many of you would say that through the years, your marriage has changed? Has your body changed? Or your hairline? Your waistline?

All of these things change over time. Change is natural. Whether you have a great marriage or a fit body, it takes a conscious effort to keep it that way.

Relationships are always either getting better or getting worse. Your heart is either growing warmer toward someone or it's growing colder. That's a fact. The same thing happens in our relationship with Christ.

There are times we don't feel as close. We just drift

apart. For one reason or another, it simply happens. So, what's the bridge to close that gap?

Be Intentional

In order to keep any relationship strong, we must be intentional. What kind of message do we send our spouse when we don't take time to strengthen our marriage? That they are on the sideline? An item not worth our time or interest? Of course, the relationship is going to weaken as a result. It has the potential of falling apart.

Think of the message you send when you are intentional—when you set down the phone, set aside your worries, problems, ideas, and distractions, and ask your spouse how their day was, and then just listen. Not only will your relationship warm up, but you'll learn more about the other person as well. However, there is a catch: it's not easy. It doesn't happen naturally. It takes discipline.

Being a *disciple* likewise takes *discipline*—after all, the two words are related. This means being a disciple requires intentionality. We have to go after our goal and do something about it. If we don't, we get into a mode of maintenance and just showing up, instead of growing in our faith—not letting our faith get stretched like God wants it to. Hebrews 2:1 tells us: "So we must listen very carefully to the truth we have heard, or we may drift away from it" (NLT).

You've probably known Christians who were on fire for the Lord, excited about their faith and being a Christian. Then, for some reason, they drifted away. You don't know where they are anymore in their faith, and they're acting like they never believed. Whatever the reason may be for their drifting, the pattern is always the same.

The Drifting Pattern

#1: Drifting from God starts when we stop giving to others, both of our time and our resources.

We are convinced that we deserve more, and we dedicate ourselves to working for more money while tightening our grip on what we already have. Jesus says that the state of our heart is directly correlated to how much we give (Mark 12:41–44). When we care for those He loves, our selfish desires dissipate. But, when we're drifting, the greatest good is acquiring things, which sometimes hurts others.

#2: Drifters stop having a devotional time.

We refuse to get up earlier or stay up late to meet with the living God. Sometimes the reasons are compelling. We get busy. Our children are sick. Our family is in crisis. No matter the reason, we stop the discipline of a devotional time.

#3: Drifters stop attending church.

We're not interested in meeting with other Christians, and hearing the Word is too convicting, so we make up excuses about the preacher and the church and choose not to go. Whatever the reason, we stop going to church, or to our small group or Bible study class.

You know you're drifting if you're in this pattern. That's the bad news; the good news is, God welcomes drifters. We're all drifters! But God brought you to this book to say, "I love you, and I welcome you back."

Sometimes we don't notice that we are drifting. There are reasons we don't see it. Yet, we are just as capable of falling away as Peter, who drifted from Jesus to the point of denying Him (Luke 22:54–62). In Peter's drifting away, we can see a few of the most common causes of our drifting away from God.

Causes of Drifting

#1: We are full of pride.

At times, we are overconfident in our relationship with the Lord. We think, "Eh, I don't need to pray about that." True, you might not say it aloud, but the way you operate in life says a lot. There are many Christians who are practical atheists: that is, they offer lip service to faith, but their actual *practice* is to go through life as if God isn't involved.

Take a look at Mark 14:27–31 (NIV):

> *"You will all fall away," Jesus told them, "for it is written: 'I will strike the shepherd, and the sheep will be scattered.' But after I have risen, I will go ahead of you into Galilee."*
>
> *Peter declared, "Even if all fall away, I will not."*

"Truly I tell you," Jesus answered, "today—yes, tonight— before the rooster crows twice you yourself will disown me three times."

But Peter insisted emphatically, "Even if I have to die with you, I will never disown you." And all the others said the same.

Peter's pride took a step forward. He basically told them all, "Everyone else is weak. Not me, Lord. I'm strong in the faith. I've got this. They will probably fall away, but not me. I'm your guy." It was a puffed-up pride that controlled his thoughts and actions.

Peter believed he was spiritually elite. First Corinthians 10:12 says: "If you think you are standing strong, be careful not to fall" (NLT).

Once we believe we know how to behave like a Christian, we begin a thought process: "I know how to play the game. I know how to get by. I know how to 'do' being a Christian." And so we just play the part, thinking the role-play is all we need to keep the label "Christian." But that's plain old hubris, which is just another way of saying "excessive pride."³ Proverbs 16:18 says: "Pride goes before destruction, a haughty spirit before a fall" (NIV). First pride, then the crash—and the bigger the ego, the harder the fall.

What can we do when the shark of pride is swirling around us and biting? Humble yourself. Get rid of ego. I say this a lot, because it's a great illustration of what ego is and what it means:

E: Edging

G: God

O: Out[4]

Whenever my ego comes into play, there's no room for God. When you say, "I don't need to do or pray about that," or "I'm too good for that," you're elevating yourself and taking God off the throne and putting yourself there.

#2: We fall asleep in our faith.

Are you tired—or worse, lazy? We've got a lot to do, and life is so busy. We get worn out because other things take priority.

Think about it this way: we only have enough time to do God's will. So, there may be things we need to cut out of our life in order to have the maximum amount of energy to focus on God's priorities for us. We are lazy when we refuse to do what we know we should do. The effect is the same.

We can start to slack off on the good habits that started our relationship with God. These little sharks, nibbling away at our good habits, drain our energy, which makes it hard to focus on God. This can happen with our marriage and our kids, and in our faith. We are concerned about other things, and they take priority over our relationship with Jesus. We forget to read God's Word, stop going to church, become lax about giving and praying—the basics.

When you forget the basics, you begin to fall away.

After Jesus and the disciples discussed who would fall

away, the disciples headed outside to the Garden of Gethsemane (Mark 14:32). Jesus asked Peter, James, and John to come inside the gates.

Then Jesus told them, His closest three, "Pray with Me. I'll go over here, but I need you to pray. I need you to be focused."

In verse 37, He came back to find Simon Peter and asked, "Simon … are you asleep? Couldn't you keep watch for one hour? Watch and pray so that you will not fall into temptation. The spirit is willing, but the flesh is weak" (Mark 14:37–38 NIV).

Doing the right thing is often hard, especially when you're exhausted. Again, that's why it takes discipline to be a disciple. Here's an example: what's easier, eating a bowl of spinach salad or a bowl of chocolate chip cookie dough ice cream?

In order to do the right thing, we need to make sure that our energy is up. My old coach used to say, "Fatigue makes cowards of us all." That is true in every area of life. We have to recharge our spiritual batteries regularly. You aren't Superman or Superwoman. You have to stay charged up. How do you maintain your spiritual energy? You get with the Lord. You have to pray.

It's not always easy—I get that. Sometimes it's not even pleasant. Nonetheless, you recharge by reading, praying, giving, serving, and being in church. Not always the easiest things to do, but they keep us from drifting. Diligence in these habits shows our priorities, and God honors your effort!

You're thinking, *"It's a discipline, and I just have to 'get into' prayer,"* yet sometimes it's like a wrestling match with a shark. Why? Because the enemy's trying to divide you from the school of fish and pull you away. Sometimes you think of praying, but you don't feel anything. It's not about feeling. It's about doing.

Then God starts to raise your energy level. He says, "Put Me first, and I'll take care of all the other stuff. You're running around, getting worn out. Let Me take care of things." How can I suggest such an absurd thing? In Matthew 6:33, He says: "Instead, be concerned above everything else with the Kingdom of God and with what he requires of you, and he will provide you with all these other things" (GNT).

Remember, every promise has a premise. The promise to have every need met is in this scripture. Put Him first, and He'll take care of the rest. Just as Peter fell asleep in the garden, we tend to fall asleep on our faith if we aren't intentional.

Fatigue is a warning sign in life. When we get tired, there is always a strong temptation to drift away. When we get worn out from everything else going on in our lives, it's easy for us to drift away from the faith. It makes us vulnerable to temptation. When you look in the Gospels, you see that Matthew recorded this same situation. Jesus' words in Matthew 26:41 are very important: "Watch and pray so that you will not fall into temptation" (NIV).

He told the disciples, in that moment, that they needed to watch and pray so that they didn't fall into temptation. Jesus knew that they were all going to walk away from the faith, but He was saying, "If you stay in prayer, if you stay connected, you'll have the strength to stand your ground in your faith."

It's the same for you. Do you need to strengthen your faith? Pray. It always comes back to prayer. Prayer is fundamental to your faith. If you play baseball, you'd better have a glove. It is a fundamental tool to playing the game. Prayer is a fundamental tool of a growing faith.

Keep in mind, if you've not prayed for some time—if you've fallen asleep—God is eager for you to awaken and to start talking with you again. Pray. *Now*. Spend some time with Him. Peter denied Jesus Christ! Yet God, in His love, still used him. He's waiting eagerly to hear your voice.

#3: We try to follow from a safe distance.

Peter feared what other people would say or think. In Mark 14, after Jesus was arrested, He was taken down into the city to await trial, and Peter went to see what was going on. But, Peter didn't want people to know that he was associated with Jesus.

It was a cold night, and a fire blazed nearby. He wandered over and held his hands over the flame. He glanced to see what they were doing with Jesus. Someone called out to Peter, asking if he was a disciple of Jesus. This person was sure he'd seen Peter following Jesus.

Peter responded adamantly, "No!" They asked again. Peter grew angry that they were asking him. He called down curses and said he did not know Jesus. That's when the rooster crowed. Peter realized his mistake. He'd denied Christ, just as Jesus had said he would. (Mark 14:66–72)

Peter was trying to follow from a safe distance, far enough back that no one would notice. We do the same sometimes. Maybe we don't do all of the godly things we used to, at least not in public anymore. We stop praying in public, over meals in the restaurant. Maybe we used to keep our Bible on our desk at work or in the truck at the job site, but we don't do that anymore. We don't know what people might think. Or, maybe we do know, and don't want to risk the consequences.

Now, having said that, it does not mean you go to the opposite extreme. Discipleship doesn't give you license to be a jerk. You can't go out and get in people's faces and tell them they're going to hell. You're not going to win anyone over that way, and you may get fired without accomplishing anything.

Instead, simply live your faith, publicly as well as privately. Jesus said to be a light (Matthew 5:15–16). How are you a light if you're always covering it up? Don't cover up the light, He said. Let it shine! Don't fear what other people think. Follow Him.

The book of Proverbs tells us, "Fear of man is a dangerous trap" (Proverbs 29:25 TLB). If we fall into the trap of hiding our faith, we start to become people-pleasers. If we're pleasing people, we can't please God. You don't want to live your life based on what other people think. That's terribly stressful and useless.

Jesus says in Mark 8:38, "If anyone is ashamed of Me, I'll be ashamed of him" (paraphrase). That's a powerful statement. Peter's desire to follow Him at a distance caused him to drift away, and it causes us to drift away as well.

When you've drifted away, and your heart's grown cold, realize God wants you back. Stop following at a distance and start making Him the priority.

How Do You Keep from Drifting Off?

Always start with *why*. Determine why you're drifting. Get to the root cause of the drifting. Why do you feel distant from the Lord? There are a multitude of reasons why we may drift.

Maybe it's one of the three reasons we've already investigated: we're trying to follow Jesus from a safe distance, or we fall asleep when it comes to our faith, or we give in to pride.

Other possible sharks that cause us to drift are:

- *Bitterness.* There is resentment lingering in your heart over something that happened long ago, or even recently.

- *Anger.* You are furious things didn't go your way. This could be about something as simple as a raise, or as painful as losing a loved one.

- *Selfishness.* Wanting everything your way is selfish, as is wanting things someone else has.

- *Pride.* Thinking only of yourself is going to get you in trouble. There's no room for God in a prideful heart.

- *Laziness.* The Bible is all the way across the room, and I'm too tired to get up and get it. But, the remote control of the TV is right here. *Click.*

Those tiny sharks pull us away. Slowly, without us knowing, they creep in. We may not even realize we are drifting. We may not even realize we're dealing with these issues, because we're doing nothing about them.

Once, we were at the beach with my family, and my youngest son was on one of the doughnut rafts. He was in the shallow water, and I watched him as he drifted along the tide. He wasn't actively swimming away from me, yet the distance between us grew.

What happened? Nothing. He just drifted. When you do nothing, you drift. Drifting always takes you in one direction—away. Sometimes we don't even notice we are drifting, but as we've already learned by Peter's example, there are deeper reasons for drifting. It helps to look at why these things happen.

Once you realized you've drifted, it's important to remember some key truths.

God Wants You Back

For some of you, He wants you for the first time. You don't have a relationship with the Lord—you don't even know what all this means—and you're just trying to figure it out. And, if you feel like you're too sinful or too messed up for God to notice you, or to love and accept you, check out this promise: the Bible tells us in Isaiah 30:18, "Yet the Lord still waits for you to come to him so he can show you his love" (TLB).

Many people think that because of all the things they've done, they can't come back to the Lord. The Bible tells us this isn't true. He's waiting for you, and He's patient. He wants to be gracious, but you're drifting further and further away. The time to come to Him is now. The reality is, if it weren't for the cross, we would all be drifting further and further away because no one would have an opportunity to come to God.

The Cross of Jesus Christ

Jesus died on the cross. He died for you and me, so that we might be saved. However, this is a gift we must actively accept. He is our Savior. He saved us from all our sins. But, we must acknowledge and accept Him as our Savior.

So, what exactly does that mean?

#1: God's love is unconditional.

Titus 3:5 tells us, "He [God] saved us—not because we were good enough to be saved but because of his kindness..." (TLB).

Many people think they have to get things straight before they get to church.

Church isn't for perfect people. People say that they don't want to be in a place that is full of hypocrites—but there's always room for one more! No one in church is perfect. Do you think that once you are a Christian, you instantly stop sinning and only do the things that please

God? That we've got life down perfectly and we're walking the way we're supposed to?

No! We're on a journey just like everyone else, and we won't be perfect until we get to heaven. But, we have help. We have Jesus. We're all just trying to make spiritual progress, not spiritual perfection.

#2: Your sin debt has been paid.

Jesus on the cross gave us a free gift. You can't work for it, and there's nothing you can do to earn it, only accept it.

First John 2:2 says: "When he [Jesus] served as a sacrifice for our sins, he solved the sin problem for good—not only ours, but the whole world's" (MSG). You have to believe that all the wrath went on Jesus on that Good Friday. If you do not believe that, then *you* have to pay for your sin and all that wrath is put on you. He took God's anger toward our sin upon Himself and brought us into fellowship with God. He bridged the gap.

#3: God doesn't hold a grudge.

People think that when bad things happen, God's punishing them for things that they've done, but that's not how God operates.

Psalm 103:9–13 says: "He never bears a grudge, nor remains angry forever. He has not punished us as we deserve for all our sins…. He has removed our sins as far away from us as the east is from the west. He is like a father to us, tender and sympathetic to those who reverence him" (TLB).

The Lord does correct us to help us along, but you're still His kid, and He loves you. If you're a parent, think about your own children who have rebelled against you or the faith. The reality is that they are still your children, and you're waiting for them to come back. Why? So you can show them your wrath? No, so you can show them your love. Some of you can understand this in personal and very painful ways.

God does the same for us. The Bible says that when we come to God, we're adopted into His family (John 1:12–13). Even when we fail Him, He doesn't turn away from us. Don't turn away from Him.

Return to God Immediately

Don't procrastinate, don't delay. Look at what Hebrews 3:15 tells us: "*Now* is the time. Never forget the warning, '*Today* if you hear God's voice speaking to you, do not harden your hearts against him'" (TLB).

Your life can change today. God is for you. Isaiah 1:18 says, "No matter how deep the stain of your sins, I [God] can take it out and make you clean as freshly fallen snow" (TLB). There's no prerequisite here. Some people say that their sin is too bad. But, the Lord wants them to come back—He wants to make them clean. You're not too far away, no matter what you've done or where you've been. No matter how far away you've drifted, it's only one step back to God.

The sharks are not more powerful than God. All it takes

is one step of saying, "I'm back, Lord. I'm here." And He will be there.

What's the next step? It's not a bunch of hoops to jump through, penance to pay and religious rules to follow. Sometimes churches and pastors complicate it, but it's really only one step, one decision.

This next verse holds a promise: "If you return to me, I will restore you so you can continue to serve me" (Jeremiah 15:19 NLT).

The good news is that Peter came back. Even after he had denied Jesus three times, Jesus Christ forgave him and got him involved (John 21:1–19). And, Peter, despite drifting away, returned. He was indeed the rock on which Jesus promised He would build His church (Matthew 16:18). Peter was still used by Jesus—and don't forget, he was someone who had completely denied Christ!

Drifting is gradual, but restoration in your relationship is immediate. Your best life begins with the decision to follow Jesus Christ more closely and intentionally. Then, you'll be equipped to overcome other weaknesses.

WORKBOOK

Chapter One Questions

Question: Have you been closer to God in the past than you are today? Evaluate the time that you spend with God, how often your heart focuses on Him, and your commitment to spiritual disciplines such as Bible reading, prayer, church involvement, and giving. Be careful of evaluating solely based on feelings, which can come and go with circumstances.

_____

_____

_____

_____

_____

_____

_____

Question: Which of the causes of drifting are you most prone to—pride, fatigue, keeping a safe distance, or one of the others mentioned? What wrong thinking or emotions keep you from acknowledging that you have drifted? How do you know that God truly wants you back?

_____

_____

_____

_____

_____

_____

_____

_____

_____

_____

_____

Journal: Write about the situations or sins that have caused you to drift away from the Lord. Renew your commitment to Him and ask Him to speak to you through this study. Accept and appreciate His forgiveness, and rejoice in your restored relationship with Him—and the future that He has for you!

_____

_____

_____

_____

_____

_____

_____

_____

_____

_____

_____

_____

_____

Action: Read or listen to the worship song "Give Me Faith" by Elevation Worship, paying special attention to the chorus. Let this powerful song encourage you as you leave behind a life of drifting and come back to God. Study the life of Simon Peter in the Gospels. At what points did he drift away, and how did Jesus restore him each time?

Chapter One Notes

_____

_____

_____

_____

_____

_____

_____

_____

_____

_____

_____

_____

_____

_____

_____

_____

_____

_____

_____

_____

_____

_____

_____

CHAPTER TWO

Don't Let Worry Drag You Down

I have a friend named Joe. One week, Joe wasn't feeling well and several of our pastors checked on him to see if he needed help. Joe admitted to us his health was failing, and we encouraged him to see the doctor.

When he arrived at the doctor's office, the nurse took him back to a room, where he waited for the physician. As the doctor entered the room, he sat on a stool and asked, "What's the problem?"

Joe crossed his arms. "I'm worried. I don't feel well."

The doctor pulled out a stethoscope and listened to Joe's breathing, then his heart. With a tiny light, he looked into his ears. The doctor then looked for a sinus infection, and he looked down Joe's throat. With a questioning expression, the doctor set the tool down and felt Joe's neck. The doctor pulled back, turned to the chart, looked over the temperature and blood pressure readings, and then set the chart down. He leaned against the wall and crossed his legs.

The doctor studied Joe for a moment and finally said, "You have nothing to worry about. You're going to live till you're 60."

"I am 60."

The doctor leaned forward. "See, I was right!"

As Joe left the doctor's office, he was more worried than when he'd arrived. If the doctor had done a thorough exam and hadn't found anything, why did he feel awful?

Joe felt a powerful draw to get to Florida. Surely, the warm state would be good for his health. He bought plane tickets to Orlando for him and his wife. But, Joe is afraid to fly—it makes him nervous. For a week before boarding the plane, he couldn't sleep.

Right before the flight, he decided to purchase a $200,000 life insurance policy. He boarded the plane, where they served him a Chinese dinner. He broke open the fortune cookie, and it read, "A recent investment will pay great dividends soon."

His mind went back to the life insurance policy he had just purchased, and beads of sweat appeared on his head. His breathing grew labored.

Joe landed in Orlando without a problem. And, despite the incredible vacation with his wife, he had a miserable time.

The fact is, like Joe, we all worry about something, but the Bible clearly tells us not to let worry control us (Philippians 4:6–7). Yet, we allow worry to control us because *we* can't control what's going on. Worry is a control issue. Worry is trying to control the uncontrollable.

The root word for *worry* in English means "to choke or strangle."[5] Isn't that how we feel when we're worrying?

We choke off breath, slowly strangling ourselves. Just like Joe, who nearly let worry kill him. He not only throttled the joy and peace out of life, but also truly made himself sick.

Near the northwestern shore of the Sea of Galilee, Jesus gave the most famous sermon in all of history, the Sermon on the Mount, found in Matthew chapters 5 to 7. Right in the heart of this message, in the midst of vital subjects, He took the time to discuss worry.

Why? Because every person who has ever existed, and those who live now, deal with worry.

Christ's Teaching on Worry

Jesus doesn't simply tell us not to worry. Just saying "stop it" won't work. Instead, He reasons with us.

That is why I tell you not to worry about everyday life—whether you have enough food and drink, or enough clothes to wear. Isn't life more than food, and your body more than clothing? Look at the birds. They don't plant or harvest or store food in barns, for your heavenly Father feeds them. And aren't you far more valuable to him than they are? Can all your worries add a single moment to your life?

And why worry about your clothing? Look at the lilies of the field and how they grow. They don't work or make their clothing, yet Solomon in all his glory was not dressed as beautifully as they are. And if God cares so wonderfully for wildflowers that are here today and thrown into the fire tomorrow, he will certainly care for you. Why do you have so little faith?

So don't worry about these things, saying, "What will we eat? What will we drink? What will we wear?" These things

> *dominate the thoughts of unbelievers, but your heavenly*
> *Father already knows all your needs. Seek the Kingdom of*
> *God above all else, and live righteously, and he will give you*
> *everything you need.*
>
> *So don't worry about tomorrow, for tomorrow will bring*
> *its own worries. Today's trouble is enough for today.*
> **—Matthew 6:25–34** (NLT)

Jesus tells us we don't need to worry, but better yet, He tells us *how* to stop worrying.

In this passage from the Sermon of the Mount, Jesus used a common Jewish argument style called the *kol wahomer*—"how much more."[6] It's a form of argument Jews used in ancient times, especially to talk about something lesser moving to something greater. In this case, it was used to point out that God obviously cares for something you might feel is less important, so His care must also extend to the more important things He looks after.

For example, birds are fed, yet they don't plant or harvest. In other words, they don't do anything to plan for and provide food for themselves. They live one day at a time, trusting they will find the food they need, because God has always provided for them. The same is true for you.

And aren't clothes even less important than food? I mean, sure, we all need clothes, but judging by the frantic way some people shop for clothing, you might think it's the most important thing in life. If God feeds the birds and clothes the fields with flowers, He will surely clothe you and take care of your needs. By contrast, worrying simply drains the fun and adventure out of life.

Four Reasons We Don't Need to Worry

#1: Worry isn't reasonable.

Matthew 6:25 says, "Do not worry about your life, what you will eat or drink; or about your body, what you will wear. Is not life more important than food, and the body more than clothes?" (NIV).

Food and clothing are relatively important, compared to some other things we pursue, but ultimately, they belong to the material sphere of life, as do vacations and large homes. I recall certain lifestyle magazines would carry alluring advertisements for champagne, cigarettes, food, clothing, antiques, carpets, exotic pillows, and even shopping trips in cities like Rome or Paris. Sound fun? Maybe.

But this materialism comes with a price. You feel as if you deserve to self-indulge—to treat yourself. But, to raise the money, you have to work hard, save hard, and possibly sacrifice your peace of mind, worrying that you won't have enough money for the fun you might have.

Our culture is out to get your money, and it longs to make you turn to self-indulgence, feeding yourself on materialism. We get stuff, and we like stuff. Yet, why is there so much anxiety? Because we feel we need more. Our acquisitions are never enough. Such narcissism is obviously unhealthy and is built on a false view of humanity—the belief that we are just soulless bodies that need to be fed, watered, clothed, and housed, and to do it as elaborately as our finances will allow.

Jesus did not teach us to despise the pleasures of life,

but He did say by implication that if we live life for pleasure, we are bound to live in slavery to the next bit of pleasure (John 8:34). We experience no increase of fun or enjoyment, but we become anxious to get the resources for more excitement.

A Christian's anxieties come from this struggle between the desire for pleasure and the satisfaction that Christ will take care of our needs. We wrestle with worry, apparently believing there's little more to life than what we eat, drink, and wear, yet say our values are above the world's values.

That's why Jesus' convicting words in Matthew 6:25 tell us life is more important than food or clothes. This passage gives us the diagnoses to our anxiety. Since life itself comes from God, why should we worry or fret about getting food or drink and the necessities of life? Jesus says He won't go halfway. He'll give you your life—He'll maintain it as long as He wills. If there's a God who has given us this great gift of life, as He has, we don't need to be anxious about the small, daily things.

So, Jesus starts right off by saying, "Do not worry. Is not life more important than food, and the body more important than clothes?" (paraphrase). Worry doesn't make sense, and it is unreasonable for a believer of Christ.

#2: Worry isn't natural.

Just from the observance of the natural world, worry is unnatural.

Matthew 6:26 says, "Look at the birds of the air; they do not sow or reap or store away in barns, and yet your heavenly Father feeds them. Are you not much more valuable than they?" (NIV).

After God says you're more valuable than birds, He keeps explaining your value. "And why do you worry about clothes? See how the flowers of the field grow. They do not labor or spin. Yet I tell you that not even Solomon in all his splendor was dressed like one of these" (Matthew 6:28–29 NIV).

Jesus was talking to a group of people for whom the struggle for survival was real. Hardly anyone was assured of their next meal. Clothes were expensive and difficult to make. There were no backup plans, no credit cards, no food banks. A famine was devastating. Thieves could destroy your life. If you did stock up on food, you were an inviting target for invaders.

How is this relevant to you? Sometimes we still worry about the necessities of life. How will I get a job to pay for the bills, put food on the table, and get a car? Perhaps a large bill is coming up, and the kids need new clothes. Or, the mortgage is high, and you just lost your job. Everyone would worry in these situations.

Jesus is saying you don't need to worry about any of it for a single second, by pointing His listeners to the surrounding birds. To the Jewish people who were just trying to make it through life, birds meant little to them. Birds were absolutely useless. They offered nothing of practical value.

Jesus is using the lesser-to-greater argument. He shows that God takes care of something that you think is useless. Don't you think He'll take care of you as well?

God takes care of birds. If He cares for them, He will

surely care for you.

The Discovery Channel has featured a documentary about a woodpecker.[7] In the show, experts perform an MRI on the woodpecker's brain. They are interested in how the brain sustains injuries, since the entire skull takes a pounding as its beak drills holes in wood. What did they find? Its brain has a shock absorber! Of course, right? God said, "I'm going to use these woodpeckers for a purpose, but they need protection. So, let's install a shock absorber in its brain." Without this small detail, woodpeckers would suffer serious brain damage. God's care for the details is incredible.

A poem by Elizabeth Cheney emphasizes this point:[8]

Said the robin to the sparrow:

"I should really like to know

Why these anxious human beings

Rush about and worry so."

Said the sparrow to the robin:

"Friend, I think that it must be

That they have no heavenly Father,

Such as cares for you and me."

Jesus goes on to point to the flowers. God carefully sculpted each flower, yet as soon as the sun gets hot, the flower melts away. If God put that much care, design, and work into flowers, don't you think He cares about the details of your life? Don't you think He's concerned about you? (I hope you never look at flowers the same way again!)

Here's the point—animals don't worry, and neither do flowers. There's only one thing in all of creation that worries: people. We're the only thing created that doesn't trust God.

God says worry isn't natural. Psalm 145:16 tells us God "satisf[ies] the desires of every living thing" (NIV). If God satisfies the desires of the ants, He'll satisfy the needs of the greater creation. He'll care for you. Worrying isn't your responsibility.

Some people say, "I'm a born worrier." No, they're not. Worry is a learned response. People learn to be a worrier from someone else. And, worry is also a practiced behavior. A baby doesn't worry about its next meal. When he's hungry, he doesn't fret. Instead, he cries. Then parents, usually the mother, acting as if God would, supply the child's needs.

As the child grows older, he is taught that it needs to prepare his own food. Does a child worry that there won't be any bread, peanut butter, and jelly? No. He simply finds the ingredients in the pantry and gets to work. And, as an adult, he works for money and buys the goods to make the sandwich. So, where does worry come in?

Imagine if a child has been told to eat the crust because there are starving children in the world. They're lucky to have a sandwich. Parents are using worry of starvation as a tool to get the child to eat. There are hundreds of little things a child can pick up—through the news, from friends and relationships, from their schooling—and all combine to create a worrying child.

We experienced the same, especially in our teens, as our needs for stronger relationships from friends created an atmosphere where we conversed about each other's worries. Anxiety about things outside our control became habitual, even diagnosable as a condition. Yet, as Christians, we're told not to worry. What are we to do?

Parents, you're modeling worry for your children. When a tough situation comes up, if you get hyper-tense and you freak out, your children are watching and learning from you. They think that when things get tough, they need to worry and stress out.

All of this worrying is unhealthy. What are the effects of worry on the body?[9] Your body isn't created to handle anxiety. So, when you worry, you take it out on your physical self. Scientific studies link worry with stomach problems, muscle ache, hyper-tension, back pain, digestive problems, and a shorter life span. Worry also leads to emotional issues, such as depression, irritability, and dread.

Now, none of this is meant to dismiss those who suffer from a chronic imbalance that creates anxiety. Even for those with a diagnosis, though, there is hope. If God has given a command not to worry, He has given a way to find peace. That's the good news.

God says worry is not natural. Since worry is learned, it can be unlearned. We'll address the remedy soon.

#3: Worry isn't helpful.

What good is worry? It doesn't change anything. It's useless. And yet, worry controls our lives. Matthew 6:27 says, "Can any of you add a single hour to your life by worrying?" (GW).

The word *add* here in the original Greek language of the Bible says it is like putting on another inch to your height. It's not up to you. Can you add a moment of time to your life by worrying? Worry isn't helpful. It doesn't add to your life—in fact, it shortens it, whereas people with peace of mind tend to live longer.

Not only does worry fail to add to your life, but it cannot change the future, either. It obviously won't change the past. So, what does worry do? It messes up today. That's all it does. It ruins your day. It puts an overwhelming weight on your heart that you carry with you, destroying your vision of the past, the hope for the future, and most importantly, your enjoyment of the now.

Proverbs 12:25 says, "Worry weighs a person down" (NLT). Nothing good comes from worry. Worry certainly doesn't make us light on our feet. In fact, it causes more fatigue, which weighs us down. Contrast the negatives of worry with Proverbs 14:30. "A heart at peace gives life to the body" (NIV). How can we have a light heart? God gives us hope.

#4: Worry isn't necessary.

Matthew 6:30 tells us why worry isn't necessary: "And if God cares so wonderfully for wildflowers that are here today and thrown into the fire tomorrow, he will certainly care for you. Why do you have so little faith?" (NLT).

Worrying is a lack of faith. Before we knew God, we had every reason for worry. We didn't know God's character. Yet, now, if you know God, you don't need to worry. Why? Because God has promised to take care of all your needs. If you trust Him, He's a father, a parent who makes sure there is peanut butter and jelly when you need it.

As a child, when I had a need, financial or otherwise, I'd go to my dad and say, "Dad, here's what I need. I need money for this or that." My dad would look over my circumstances carefully, measure my needs, and suggest, "Get a job." While he was typically joking, because I was too young to actually get a job, I knew he would supply most of my needs, but I had to work for others, depending on what my character required. He always wanted to make sure I knew the value of hard work. But, especially when it came to things like Little League Baseball fees, clothes for school, or food, in all my years growing up, I never once worried about where my dad was going to get the money to care for me.

Yet, for my own growth, I had to work. I knew he wanted me out of the house for a few hours and to bring in some resources to pay for the things I wanted. Yet, for the vitals, I knew he would come up with the money. It's a dad/kid kind of thing. Kids ask, dads provide judiciously. I never worried at all. I just figured he'll know where to get resources. That's his job.

Similarly, with our Heavenly Father, He already knows our needs. If you come to Christ and say, "Lord, I want

You to be number one in my life. I want to live for You. I want to follow Your plan," then God will assume responsibility for all the needs in your life. He has a plan. A path. Philippians 4:19 says, "God will meet all your needs … in Christ Jesus" (NIV).

All your needs. In the Greek, in the context, *all* actually means "all."[10] Simple. It doesn't mean some, partial, or even just the things you can't take care of yourself. It means everything. God will meet all your needs in Christ. Does that include bills? Does that include your relationship needs? Your financial needs? Does that include your housing needs?

Yes—*all*.

What are we saying, then, when we worry? Is God a liar? Rare is the moment someone would dare suggest such a thing. If we're followers of Christ and if He's promised us all of these things, is He a liar? No. Proof says He's never lied (Hebrews 6:18). Sometimes we act like He lies by letting worry cloud our judgment and enjoyment of Him.

The bottom line is that worry is misunderstanding God's character. Anytime you start worrying, there should be alarm bells in your mind that say, "Something's off here. I've forgotten who God is and that He's with me all the time." Alarm bells mean you're just focused on yourself. You believe that you have to handle it alone. However, God is a loving father who cares about your needs and you need to refocus on Him.

Worry is a progressive line. If you don't know what God is like, then you won't trust Him. If you don't trust God, the bottom line is that you will live a life of worry.

And, when worry controls your life, there's no room for trust and faith. They can't coexist. They're oil and water.

Many people say, "Well, I trust Jesus for my salvation, but I still worry." Think about how illogical that is. I trust Jesus Christ for my biggest problem, He's getting me out of hell and into heaven. My eternal punishment is paid for, but I don't trust Him for this smaller issue that I have going on today.

Everything else is miniscule compared to what He's already given us—we're washed, pure, given a purpose for living.

Jesus gives us so many reasons to stop worrying. Yet, we all worry. It's time to be practical and get down to where we live. How do you stop worrying?

How to Stop Worrying

Most people would agree that worrying is a problem, but how do you stop it? Turning the tide against the sharks of worry takes some practice. Remember, you must unlearn all you've learned. This takes time.

The antidote isn't telling yourself not to worry. That kind of self-talk simply produces guilt and leads to self-loathing. Instead, practice these four adjustments God gave us from the Sermon on the Mount. Among other things, they'll help you understand why God's words are important to begin with.

#1: Get to know God.

Matthew 6:32 says, "People who don't know God and

the way he works fuss over these things" (MSG).

Knowing God is foundational. Learning about Him is what everything else is built on.

If you don't know God, if you don't have a relationship with Him, you *should* worry. There's very real trouble here. If you don't know God, you're on your own. You've given the enemy free rein. You live your whole life to the natural so that you forget there's a whole spiritual life, too. When you say yes to Jesus Christ, there's a transaction that happens, a covenant. You belong to Him. And, God takes care of you. He assumes responsibility for you. He stands in front of you, and if the devil is coming for you, he has to go through Christ. Satan can't win.

Get that relationship with God; otherwise, you're an easy target.

If you're a Christian, worry is practical atheism. Every time you're worrying, you're acting like there is no God. You're acting like every aspect of life all depends on you and not God. You act as if you don't believe God will keep His promises.

When you worry, you might as well be an unbeliever, because you're saying that it's all up to you.

I have a friend who always asks me, "Hey, how are you? How's the family? Ministry going okay? What have you been up to? Been feeling okay? Working hard? How can I pray for you?" He's one of those. If I can finally get a word in, I'll ask him, "Well, how are you?"

I like him.

He's one of those guys who hates talking about himself. It's refreshing. This is what he said to me: "I'm great. I mean, I have cancer, so I'd appreciate it if you'd pray for that, but—"

I go, "*What?* You have cancer?"

He admits, "Yeah, it's not a big deal."

I proceeded to ask him what stage and so forth.

He said, "Well, they might take out the prostate, but with people my age, it doesn't matter." He's just brushing it off. He tells me that he's blessed. He says that God will either heal him or He won't. He adds solemnly, "I'd feel bad for my family, but I'd go to a better place. I'm excited for it at some point, if the cancer's not that serious, that's great, too."

He's so nonchalant, and I realize that it's such a great attitude. He's not worried one bit. If worry will shorten your life, then his lack of worry will help him in his healing. And then, when he's around non-believers and they hear his attitude, what a witness!

When you're around people and they're watching you, they observe your worry, and at the end of the day, they wonder what the point of faith is. Worry doesn't work when times are hard—you can't lean on it. So, they may ask, what's the point of God?

When we have an attitude of trusting God and knowing that the Lord gives and takes away (Job 1:21), when we're not worrying about the past or the future problems, that's a huge witness to those who don't know the Lord. They get a glimmer of who God is and the point of worshiping Him.

The more you get to know God, the more you can handle these things.

Let's turn to the Sermon on the Mount. If you want to stop worrying, here's the next step:

#2: Put God first in every area of your life.

Matthew 6:31–33 says: "So do not worry.... But seek first his kingdom and his righteousness, and all these things will be given to you as well" (NIV).

I recently gave a commencement message at my alma mater, San Diego Christian College, and I ended with this verse because it says everything you need. When you leave college, you're worried about providing for yourself, getting a job, and getting out in the world. Put God first and He'll take care of the rest.

Any time you take God out of the center of your life and put anything else in His place, it's not going to go well. If God is your center, there's nothing else that can fit. People look all their lives for something to be there. And, if they don't find God, there's nothing that will help.

This works like a wheel. God's supposed to be the center, the hub. Everything else in your life is a spoke. We often put God as a spoke in our life and we take Him out of the hub and replace it with something else.

Your hub is what you spend the most time thinking about, your obsession. The only thing that's supposed to be there is God. Nothing else can handle being in the hub. When you allow anything else to take first place in your life, anytime you love anything more than God, you're going to be victimized by worry. God designed you in such a way as to have Him as your hub, the center of your life. He didn't design you to live with worry.

#3: Live one day at a time.

Summed up, Matthew 6:34 says, "Give your entire attention to what God is doing right now, and don't get worked up about what may or may not happen tomorrow. God will help you deal with whatever hard things come up when the time comes."

Notice that Jesus doesn't say you can't plan for tomorrow. We should plan ahead. But, if we're always living in planning mode, we miss today's blessings. If you're always thinking about tomorrow, you can't enjoy today.

When you're always worried about tomorrow, the future is overwhelming. There's no way to know all the problems you'll face the rest of your life. There are always going to be problems. We get them in twenty-four-hour segments called days that come in bite-sized pieces. Jesus will you give you the strength for the day. Matthew 6:11 says, "Give us today our daily bread" (NIV). Not our weekly food, but our daily bread.

Worry and trust cannot fit in the same heart. We have to constantly be pushing out that worry and pulling in the trust. Don't give up. It must be learned.

#4: Remember that God cares for you.

Through everything you're going through, remember that God cares about the details of your life and the things you're dealing with. Matthew 6:31–32 says not to worry, because your Father in heaven knows all your needs.

And He never takes a moment off from watching over you. He's never too busy or half-asleep so that He misses something. First Peter 5:7 says, "Let him have all your worries and cares, for he is always thinking about you and watching everything that concerns you" (TLB). This powerful verse is worth memorizing. When you're feeling forgotten by God and when you're feeling left out, this one is great to recite.

In Daniel chapter 3, three men, Shadrach, Meshach, and Abednego would not bow to the king, and he threw them into a fiery furnace. There are some things you'll notice with this story. God could have saved them from going into the flames. Instead, God led them *to* the fire. God led them *through* the fire. And, Jesus was with them *in* the fire. The fire didn't harm them.

Some of you might be going through difficulties and feel like you're in the middle of the fire. You might think it's a punishment, as if it's something that God is doing to you because of something bad you did, but that's not the reality.

If you're going through the fire right now, God's not trying to punish you, He's trying to promote you. Shadrach, Meshach, and Abednego went through the fire and were unharmed. They were promoted. They went on to be trusted with great things.

Can You Go Through the Fire and Not Worry?

There are two practical ways to get through times of trouble without worrying.

The first is to memorize Scripture. Philippians 4:13 is a good place to start: "For I can do everything through Christ, who gives me strength" (NLT). Repeating these words through times of trial can give you strength and put Christ back in the center, as your hub. The promise comes in and the worry is expelled.

This is like an insurance policy for believers. When I get an insurance policy, I read what the policy says. Then, once I know what's covered, I don't worry about it anymore.

The reason you're worrying is that you don't know what's covered in life. You haven't read God's insurance policy. You haven't looked at the promises. Memorize and bring the promises with you through the fire.

The second practical way to keep from worrying is prayer. It's the key to your strength, your vitality, your peace, and your joy.

Philippians 4:6–7 says, "Don't worry about anything; instead, pray about everything. Tell God what you need, and thank him for all he has done. Then, you will experience God's peace, which exceeds anything we can understand. His peace will guard your hearts and minds as you live in Christ Jesus" (NLT).

The reality is that if you prayed as much as you worried, you'd have a lot less to worry about. If it's not worth praying about, it's not worth worrying about.

Keep these things in mind as you move forward in your life. Making Christ your hub and keeping the rest in the spokes while focusing on prayer and memorization means you have the tools to move worry out of your life and fill it with faith and trust. With this solid foundation, sharks swirling about you will see you're stronger than they are. Because you are.

Chapter Two Questions

Question: What things in your life do you tend to worry about the most? Describe a time when worry hindered you from fully enjoying the blessings that you have or from fully embracing God's plan for you.

_____

_____

_____

_____

_____

_____

_____

_____

_____

_____

Question: What are some practical ways you can get to know God more deeply? Is God first in your life, or have you made something else your center (e.g., marriage, career, parenting, church, leisure activities)? What worries in this part of your life could be resolved by committing yourself to God's preeminence over it and His lordship over all of your life? How can you trust God more and follow Him one day at a time?

_____

_____

_____

_____

_____

_____

_____

_____

_____

_____

_____

Journal: Write down a list of reasons why you can trust God, and stories from your own life of times when you have seen God's provision and protection over you. How do you know that God cares about you? How should that change how you live?

_____

_____

_____

_____

_____

_____

_____

_____

_____

_____

_____

_____

Action: Look back at the verses on worry in this chapter. Choose at least one verse or passage to memorize, and ask God to bring it to your mind when you begin to worry. Use that verse in prayer when you are feeling anxious or uncertain.

Chapter Two Notes

CHAPTER THREE

Identify the Bait

The shallow bay is calm and clear and of perfect temperature. The only ripples are made by tall shark fins cutting through the water. A closer look reveals dozens of sharks swirling under the surface.

No matter. You kick off your flipflops and prepare to dive in. As you approach the edge, you scrape your toe, and it starts to bleed. Well, no matter. It should stop bleeding while you swim. You dive in the water.

Something brushes by your leg, and you suddenly realize this was a bad idea. But, swimming in the alluring water was just too tempting.

Sometimes we know there's danger, and yet, we are still lured in, swimming with the deceptions we've told ourselves and whatever danger the devil can bring.

The oldest problem in the world is temptation. Eve was tempted in the garden to take a bite of the forbidden fruit, and Adam followed right behind her. Their children fell into temptation, leading to murder. But even before, an angel was tempted to rebel against God, and was cast out of heaven. That angel was Satan. So, when I say temptation is the oldest problem, I mean it truly is the original issue.

The definition of *temptation* in the Oxford English Dictionary is "the desire to do something, especially something wrong or unwise."[11] Wanting to jump into a bay of hungry sharks is a temptation that is very unwise.

Remember how Jesus spoke about temptation in Matthew 26:41: "Watch and pray so that you will not fall into temptation. The spirit is willing, but the flesh is weak" (NIV).

In our spirit, we want to beat temptation. We want to live for God and be spiritually minded. We want to be on fire for the Lord and walking with Him. Yet, there's a humanness to us that will always be weak in the flesh. Our flesh longs for those things that are wrong and unwise, while our spirit wants to overcome. So, how are we to overcome the temptation? The more we're connected to Christ, the less we'll give in to temptation. In other words, we're to create a stronger relationship with Christ so that we overcome temptation.

Jesus Christ acknowledges our frailty. How can He know our temptation so well? Because He was both human and God, taking on the temptations we know so well. The Message paraphrase says it like this: "Stay alert; be in prayer so you don't wander into temptation without even knowing you're in danger. There is a part of you that is eager, ready for anything in God. But there's another part that's as lazy as an old dog sleeping by the fire" (Matthew 26:41). He overcame temptation, so when He offers this advice, we need to take it.

Temptations are designed by the devil in order to cause you to fall down. The purpose is to draw us away from God and lead us into sin. These temptations are designed to expose us and our weaknesses, and if our shortcomings aren't worked on, they have the potential to separate us from God. Like the sharks that circle in the water, Satan is eager to get us to leave the safety of the school so we're easy prey.

How Do We Resist Temptation?

James 4:7 says, "Resist the devil and he will flee from you." Excellent! Resisting the devil is key to avoiding giving into temptation. But, what does resisting entail?

First Corinthians 10:13 (NLT) explains:

> *The temptations in your life are no different from what others experience. And God is faithful. He will not allow the temptation to be more than you can stand. When you are tempted, he will show you a way out so that you can endure.*

In part, resisting means we're to endure. Endurance doesn't have the connotation that something's fun or pleasant: *Hang in there, hold out, be strong. You'll get through.*

Here's the thing about bait and lures. Whatever temptation trips you up has hooks in it. Every single bait and every single lure has hooks. So, how do we not take the bait and bite?

7 Keys to Overcoming the Lure of Temptation

#1: You have to be realistic.

Temptation is going to happen. As the verse in Corinthians tells us, it's not *if* you'll be tempted—it's *when*.

We have to face the fact that we'll be tempted. I talk to Christians all the time who tell me they feel terrible when tempted by this or that. They think they can't do this Christianity thing because they feel the temptation to sin. The reason you're tempted is because you're a human being. You have to ease up on yourself a little bit when you're tempted.

You're going to want to speak your mind. You're going to want to yell at your kids. You're going to want to flip on a video game instead of doing your homework. You're going to want to tell the secret someone just trusted you with. Those temptations are a part of life. You must resist.

The reality is the more committed you are to Jesus Christ, the more often you will be tempted. Either way, as a Christian, you will be tempted.

#2: You have to be responsible.

James 1:13 warns us, "And remember, when you are being tempted, do not say, 'God is tempting me.' God is never tempted to do wrong, and he never tempts anyone else" (NLT).

You might wonder why God would put certain things in front of you. You might ask why He put you in your current situation. But, that's passing off responsibility. He didn't put you in your situation—you put yourself there. You turned on that channel. You went to that website. You called your friend to tell them the secret. You flirted with a person despite having commitments. That was you.

For example, temptation for adultery is all around us these days. You can't push off the responsibility and say, "Well, why was that woman or man in my life? Why did God put them in my neighborhood, at my job, or at the gym?" God didn't put her or him there. Take responsibility for placing yourself in the situation. If you're blaming everyone else, you will dull your sense of responsibility and power to overcome temptation.

What's my biggest problem in avoiding temptation? It's me. *I'm* my biggest problem. Walk over to a mirror right now and peek at the reflection. Your biggest problem is the person in the glass.

We all have issues in our past, and we all have people that have caused issues in our lives. You might admit to yourself that you didn't get a fair shake at life. Your parents were a certain way and there was a person in your life that did something. You can go through the whole list and keep blaming everyone else, but at some point, you realize that the reason this is happening is due to your focus. It's your responsibility to control your reactions. How you respond is what you can control. You can't control temptation, but you can control the environment you put yourself in, and you can control what you focus on.

Don't play the blame game. Whenever you blame, you lose the effectiveness of avoiding temptation. If you take responsibility, you can move forward.

#3: You have to be aware.

Second Corinthians 2:9–11 (NIV) says:

> *Another reason I wrote you was to see if you would stand the test and be obedient in everything. Anyone you forgive, I also forgive. And what I have forgiven—if there was anything to forgive—I have forgiven in the sight of Christ for your sake, in order that Satan might not outwit us. **For we are not unaware of his schemes.*** *(emphasis added)*

Know your own desires. The Bible tells us we need to be prepared for temptation. Mastery of self is key here. Knowing yourself is the key to controlling yourself.

You have to know yourself to know what tempts you, to know how you will respond to certain temptations, so that you can be on guard. Temptation isn't going to give us a warning that at 8 p.m. tonight, it's coming to tempt us with a movie, a website, or even a person. So, you have to know what bait causes you to bite.

Temptation is simply taking a legitimate, natural desire and trying to fulfill it an illegitimate and counterfeit way. In other words, Satan takes a routine desire and turns it into a runaway desire. It's a normal part of life, but all of a sudden, it's the only thing you can think about.

You know you've been hooked when it's all you can think about. Even God-given desires, out of control, become destructive.

So, you need to know your triggers and have a plan to avoid those situations. Don't put yourself in their path, in the same way you wouldn't jump in a beautiful bay of perfect water with a bunch of sharks and expect not to get bitten. What are the things that cause you to fall? Know what they are. Triggers aren't the same for everyone. Bait looks different for everyone. Although they might come from common situations, there are certain things that tempt you that don't me, and vice versa.

One area where this is key is leadership. When we're looking for leaders, we're looking for humility and self-discipline. Every person must lead themselves. If you can't control yourself, you can't have effective friendships, families, or lead other people.

For another example, let's look at dating. You're a raging hormone factory, eager to spend time with the person you like. But, you must have a plan to overcome your glands. Even as an adult, it's the same issue. You need a plan before it's too late.

#4: You have to understand the process.

How do you prepare for temptation? You prepare for it by understanding temptation. The only good thing you can say about the devil is this: he's consistent. He's still using the same old tricks he's been using for thousands and thousands of years. He uses a process. There are common temptations with common solutions.

Let's look at 2 Corinthians 2:11, which says, "After all, we don't want to unwittingly give Satan an opening for yet more mischief—we're not oblivious to his sly ways!" (MSG).

What are his sly ways? He grabs your attention and

uses your imagination.

You notice the temptation, then you let your imagination play. How can I get away with this? How can I make it work? The temptation is something you have an inclination toward. Once it grabs your imagination, you start to get a feeling, and the more you imagine, the more your emotionally invested in the temptation. Wouldn't it be fun to shop right now? You could hang out at the mall, that glorious place with the lights and smells and people. Sure, you don't have money, but you won't buy anything. You imagine walking and shopping, and before you know it, you're running up a debt on your credit cards.

Pretend you like a person other than your spouse. You imagine spending time with them, maybe on a date. Where could that lead? You've completely forgotten about your spouse. Then, imagination turns into a feeling. There's a desire to create a make-believe relationship—what's the harm of fantasy? Because it's not harmless! The feeling leads to flirting that leads to rising affections of some form. No fantasy is harmless. What you flirt with, you will eventually fall for. Count on it. What starts in your mind eventually comes out in your behavior in some form.

Here's an exercise. Close your eyes and imagine you have a lemon in your hand. Now, you're going to want to have someone read this next part to you to get the full effect. (But even if you don't have someone else readily available, you'll still get the point from reading it yourself.)

The cool touch of the peel is the first thing you sense. The exterior is tough, smooth, and rubbery. Feel the two lumps on the ends? Okay, now open your eyes and take a knife and cut the lemon in half. Careful—don't cut yourself. Oh, look at the juices running down over the sides! Wow, the smell of the lemon's fresh juice is strong. Now, put one half down and just hold the other half of the lemon. It's such a happy color yellow.

Now squeeze the lemon. See the juice ooze up and cover the surface of the cut lemon? Now lick the lemon. That's right! Lick the lemon. Who feels like you have more saliva than you did a minute ago?

How can that be? It was only pretend! The reason is because your body reacts to what your mind thinks about.

Just a little harmless fantasy? It's not harmless. Your imagination is always leading you toward what you are thinking about. What starts out in your mind always leads to action, which leads to this last point.

If you're thinking of something all the time, eventually, it'll come out in your life. What you flirt with, you'll eventually fall for, and after you fall for it, you'll be fighting for your integrity, your job, your marriage, your self-respect. Temptations can ruin you if you allow your imagination to run wild.

We live so immersed in the natural world that we forget about the spiritual. The devil wants to destroy you. He doesn't want to mess around with you—he wants to eliminate you. The only reason you haven't been destroyed yet is because God has protected you and is patient with you and me. We have to give our lives over to the Lord, more and more, in a process of surrendering to Him.

As James 4:7 instructs us, "Resist the devil, and he will

flee from you" (NIV). He'll realize you're a lost cause because you've resisted him.

So, what's your weak spot? What's your bait? What's luring you? What has your attention? Maybe you've just realized that you have to give your weaknesses over to the Lord. Maybe you haven't turned what you are imagining into an action yet, but the things you watch, read, and listen to are being uploaded into your mind and will soon come out in your behavior.

#5: You have to realize the result.

It's time you recognize the result of giving into temptation. James 1:15 says, "These desires give birth to sinful actions. And when sin is allowed to grow, it gives birth to death" (NLT). Desires to sin to death—it's a pattern that escalates quickly.

The tragic part of sin is that you can't get away from the consequences of your actions. Sin eventually comes with all the consequences it can bring. Death of a marriage, a relationship, a job, a dream, and maybe your faith, which is the opposite of what God has planned for you. And, worst of all, physical death sometimes accompanies a fallen pattern of sin.

You're free to choose any lifestyle you want, but you're not free to choose the consequences of that free-will decision. The consequences are set.

Look at 1 Corinthians 6:12: "You say, 'I am allowed to do anything'—but not everything is good for you. And even though 'I am allowed to do anything,' I must not become a slave to anything" (NLT).

That's the lure you don't want to bite on, because suddenly you become a slave to whatever you've fallen into. Like a fisherman with a fish on the line, you'll go wherever it leads. The temptation has hooked your mouth. You can't stop.

The moment I make the choice to bite, I'm no longer free. You can go to the top of the Empire State Building, and there's the freedom to jump off. What if someone asks on the way down, "How's it going?" Of course, you seem to be falling okay. "So far, so good," you respond, because you're still alive and the fall is thrilling. However, there are consequences coming, otherwise known as the ground.

That's where many people are right now. They're in the middle of being hooked, in the middle of a temptation. They're halfway down, and if someone were to ask them, they'd say, "So far so good!" But the ground is coming.

That's the reality of life. You can try to change the consequences, but it won't help. They will win.

I won't break the law of gravity if I jump off the building, and just because I feel like I'm flying free doesn't mean this is going to end well. It just means that the law of gravity is going to break me. We don't break God's laws; at the end of the day, if we follow temptation, they break us.

Many haven't hit bottom yet, so they don't realize the consequences. There's a cause and effect. Laws and principles in God's Word are not there to harm or restrict you, they are there to help you. When in doubt, grab the manual and get in the instruction book. When you sin, you don't just hurt God. You hurt yourself.

It's like a train on railroad tracks. It's pointless to think that the tracks are dumb. Why stew because the tracks don't lead where you want to go? The train can't jump off the tracks safely. The train *needs* the tracks. Similarly, a Christian needs the tracks, such as God's Word, church, prayer, and devotions. Jumping off the tracks will cause problems—a train wreck.

God's telling us that He has given us these things to keep us safe, to keep us going, and to get us where He wants us to go. If we stay on the tracks, we'll have joy and fulfillment. You'll get further than you could by hating them or even jumping off the tracks.

You are free to choose your response, but the moment you choose what you're going to do with your life and your lifestyle, you are no longer free. Jump into the water with sharks and you're going to get bit.

The Bible is saying you need to handle temptation— we're all tempted—and there are some common solutions: Stay on the tracks. Stay focused on Him.

Temptation is going to happen. It's part of life. It doesn't mean you're bad; it means you're human.

#6: You have to refocus your mind.

How do we restructure our mind to avoid temptation? A simple fear of sharks doesn't keep people from swimming near them. What does God say?

Romans 12:2 says, "Let God transform you into a new person by changing the way you think. Then you will learn to know God's will for you, which is good and pleasing and perfect" (NLT).

It's going to take a serious change of thinking to avoid temptation. You are going to have to be a new person.

Look at Psalm 119:9, which says, "How can a young person stay on the path of purity? By living according to your word" (NIV). And, 1 Corinthians 10:13 says, "When you are tempted, he will show you a way out so that you can endure" (NLT).

Since temptation begins in your mind, changing your mind is the key to overcoming temptation. If you want to overcome temptation, you have to redirect your thoughts. Use the replacement principle. When you're holding a doughnut in your hand, what you shouldn't do is tell yourself not to eat it because you will. You don't keep telling yourself not to, not to, not to. You must replace it with something. Put down the doughnut, back away, and get something else.

Telling young men not to think about women constantly is another example: "Don't have impure thoughts about women. Stop thinking about them. Are you thinking about them in skimpy clothes? Did you have an immodest thought? Stop thinking about women!" Bombarded by those kinds of admonitions, *all* men are going to be able to think about is women!

Replace impure thoughts with the Word, prayer, and a relationship with God. Help out at church, in the community, and at home. Find hobbies on which to spend your energies. In short, focus on healthy things. All of these things keep you on the tracks.

Sometimes, in certain situations, you just have to get up and leave. Get out of there! Change the mental channel. Change your mind. Change what you're thinking about.

Refocus your thoughts.

That's the point. Instead of focusing on what you don't want, focus on what you do want. Refocus on what's positive and good and perfect. Redirect your attention.

#7: You have to get a fresh start on life.

We fall into habits—some good, some bad. Some keep the sharks away. Others seem to invite them.

Not all is lost if you've fallen into temptation. If you want to break a bad habit, this is the most important principle. The key is God's power in your mind. We're never so far gone that we can't get a fresh start.

James 4:7 tells us, "Submit yourselves, then, to God" (NIV). This is about spiritual rebirth. There is a definite moment, a specific time when you commit your life to Christ and say, "Jesus Christ, help me out. Take my life. I want You to be number one in my life." If you haven't done this, you need to call out to Him. Maybe you've been thinking about it for weeks or months or years. Now is the time.

Maybe it's confusing to you and you don't understand what being born again means. When you're born, you get a fresh start in life. Being born again means a new life in Christ, a fresh start in life. Second Corinthians 5:17 says, "This means that anyone who belongs to Christ has become a new person. The old life is gone; a new life has begun!" (NLT).

I love thinking that God takes an enormous blackboard and writes on it the specifics of everything I've ever done wrong, that I feel guilty for, and what I regret. Then, I say,

"God, take my life, all of it—the good, the bad, the ugly! Jesus Christ, just save me!" At this, He takes a big eraser and erases the whole thing. He wipes the slate clean. I get a new start, a new life. I'm reborn. And, together we draw out a new path, a new plan.

We need to be reborn in order to have God's power in our lives.

You say you're trying, but it isn't working. Will-power, self-help books, Oprah, hoping you'll change—they don't work. All they show is that people are searching. It might give you the principles, but it doesn't give you the power. Or, perhaps you're a Christian, but what you need is a rededication. How many of you tried to get your act together, tried to get your life in order before you became a Christian? Did it work? Not really. The reason why you still have those habits and hang-ups and hassles that are still holding on to you is because there is an area of your life you have not yet given totally to Jesus Christ.

You need God's power, a power beyond yourself, to come in and help you change. Jesus Christ gives us the power to change our lives.

Being born again gives you a new capacity to resist temptation. You will not really be able to say *no* to the things you know are harmful to you until first you've said *yes* to God. I'm not talking about a religion. I'm not talking about going to church. I'm not talking about being a nice person, confirmed, or baptized. I'm talking about saying to Jesus, "Take me as I am and use me!"

Out of Control and into His Command

Where are you most vulnerable to temptation? Where are your weak spots? What areas are so out of control in your life that you just can't seem to gain control? Is it your temper? Your speech? Is it your eating, sex drive, spending, dissatisfaction, envy, drinking—what's out of control?

It's time to become a new person, which begins with admitting that you have a problem. God is a hospital for sinners. The good news is that you can change with the power of Jesus Christ. There are people who are living proof of it, and they are eager to share their story.

I'm not saying He's going to change you into a fanatic or a weirdo, or someone who's standing on the street corner with a sign declaring that the world will end, "so repent!" But the reality is, when you give your life to Him, He makes you more in your right mind.

Everyone needs a fresh start at some point. Now is the time to become born again. Reach out to Him. God will give you control over your habits and put you under His wings of protection. I'm not saying you'll never be tempted, because you will, but you'll be able to recognize the bait—and you won't jump into the water full of sharks.

WORKBOOK

Chapter Three Questions

Question: What are the greatest temptations that you face? What particular sins tempt you? In what situations are you most likely to be tempted? What emotions (e.g., loneliness or exhaustion) cause you to feel greater temptation than usual? What bait really draws you in? Is there something that you spend a lot of time imagining and fantasizing about? Do you have any other personal triggers?

_____

_____

_____

_____

_____

_____

_____

_____

Question: Consider the temptations you recognized in the previous question. What would your life look like if you gave in to each one? What freedom would you trade for the slavery of sin? What consequences will or could follow? Who would be hurt if you gave into temptation?

_____

_____

_____

_____

_____

_____

_____

_____

_____

_____

_____

Journal: Write down three temptations that you are currently battling, and then a replacement thought pattern for each one. Is there a verse you can claim over that temptation, or a spiritual discipline that will help you to refocus your mind and life? Do you need to change some habits and associations?

_____

_____

_____

_____

_____

_____

_____

_____

_____

_____

_____

_____

Action: Share your testimony with a Christian mentor and ask them to give you insight into how you can live out, on a daily basis, the fact that you are dead to sin and alive to God. If you have questions about being born again as described in this chapter, talk to a pastor or other biblically grounded Christian leader who can help you be sure of your salvation and understand what it means.

Chapter Three Notes

CHAPTER FOUR

Don't Complain About the Water

You must go in the water. You're filthy and tired, and you dropped your wedding ring into the swimming pool. You can see it glimmering at the bottom. There are no sharks. Yet, what if there were freshwater sharks? Like when you were a kid and your dad was swimming underwater toward you.

And what's worse, the water is probably cold. And, once you get in, you'll get all wet, and then you'll have to dry off. Why do you have to go in? You hate this, so much.

It's easy to read the story of the person above and tell them to stop complaining and just get in the water and get the ring. It's a wedding ring, for goodness' sake, and getting wet is no big deal. Stop whining and jump in.

Yet, we complain about our own circumstances all the time, looking silly to the people around us and killing the joy of ourselves and others.

> *Do everything without complaining and arguing, so that no one can criticize you. Live clean, innocent lives as children of God, shining like bright lights in a world full of crooked and perverse people.*
> **—Philippians 2:14–15** *(NLT)*

We want to be transparent and real, not fake, not putting up a mask. But, we try to show our best. Why is that? The Bible doesn't gloss over heroes. It shows their faults and weaknesses, and I'm glad. It's one way we know it's the Word of God, because if it wasn't from God, it would only show us the rosy and good things about our heroes. It would never show the reality of their humanity.

Here's the reality—complaining is a killjoy. It affects you and those around you. "I love being around people who complain," said no one ever. It's negativity that's unneeded and it impacts everyone.

Scientists are figuring out that the Bible gives great scientific advice. When God said over two thousand years ago that complaining is bad for you, He wasn't kidding.

Dr. Travis Bradberry, author of *Emotional Intelligence 2.0*, shares about the physical effects of complaining:[12]

Scientists like to describe this process as, "Neurons that fire together, wire together." Repeated complaining rewires your brain to make future complaining more likely. Over time, you find it's easier to be negative than to be positive, regardless of what's happening around you. Complaining becomes your default behavior, which changes how people perceive you. And here's the kicker: complaining damages other areas of your brain as well. Research from Stanford University has shown that complaining shrinks the hippocampus—an area of the brain that's critical to problem solving and intelligent thought.

Damage to the hippocampus is scary, especially when you consider that it's one of the primary brain areas destroyed by Alzheimer's.

Negativity is a muscle that can grow stronger and stronger. No matter what's going on, you'll be well practiced in finding negativity. The more you complain, the stronger the neurological bonds grow. No exaggeration, you may be making yourself more susceptible to brain diseases by complaining:[13]

When you complain, your body releases the stress hormone cortisol. All the extra cortisol released by frequent complaining impairs your immune system and makes you more susceptible to high cholesterol, diabetes, heart disease and obesity. It even makes the brain more vulnerable to strokes.

Save your brain and your health by listening to what the Bible has to say.

Yet, complaining is a hard habit to break. So many people seem to be naturally negative. We tend to look at the bad things in life and savor them. In this, we are conditioned by society. What makes headlines? Bad news. "If it bleeds, it leads," because people want to see the blood, the gore, the unique and bizarre. The inexplicable gets ratings. We are bombarded continuously with what's wrong with everything. By our own nature and by our conditioning, we tend to develop the habit of complaining until it becomes our default.

This is one of the main reasons so many people don't

go to church. Eighty-five percent of churches are dying.[14] Why? There's so much negativity. The church in America has become known for what it's against. What if we were known for what we're for, like helping others? Instead of complaining about the issues in our community, let's serve them. Instead of complaining about the government, let's pray for it. When it comes to the issue of complaining, the Bible says that God wants Christians to be different. That means less complaining.

What does God's Word have to say about dealing with this habit of complaining? The Bible describes four common types of complainers.

#1: The Whiner

These people wake up negative. They don't rise and shine—instead, they rise and whine.

There's a biblical example of this very problem. King David was a man after God's own heart (Acts 13:22). He was a strong saint, but he had an issue with whining. If you read his psalms, you see a lot of complaining: "Have I been wasting my time? Why take the trouble to be pure? All I get out of it is trouble and woe—every day and all day long!" (Psalm 73:13–14 TLB).

David was analyzing the world and saw evil people prospering. Why were they successful and evil when David was trying to be pure? Yet by the end of the chapter, he figures it out. In verse 28, he says, "But as for me, I get as close to him as I can! I have chosen him, and I will tell everyone about the wonderful ways he rescues me" (TLB). No matter how evil the world is, he would choose God.

The Bible has more examples of whiners. An employer hired workers in the morning, and more in the middle of the day, and even more at the end of the day. After work, he paid them all equal wages. The ones hired in the morning weren't happy. Matthew 20:11–12 says, "They took their money and started grumbling against the employer. '...[W]e put up with a whole day's work in the hot sun— yet you paid them the same as you paid us!'" (GNT).

We don't know if it was agreed that these last workers would come back the next day to earn the rest of the money, but all we know is that Jesus pointed out there was a price agreement, and the men decided they didn't like it, and the men started complaining to their employer. They shouldn't have been whining about their pay since they had agreed on an amount.

Favorite phrases of the whiner are: "It's not fair! I don't deserve this! Everyone else gets all the breaks!" This creates a motif that drains the world of joy.

Here's the reality: life isn't fair, and God never said it would be. In fact, He warns Job life is terribly unfair. Yet, it will be fair in heaven. God will settle the score in heaven and hell, but until then, it's not fair. As long as you complain about that, it will only make you and the people around you more miserable. Whining will never change the facts.

#2: The Martyr

A biblical example of a martyr is Moses. The book of Numbers records that "Moses said to the Lord, 'Why pick on me, to give me the burden of a people like this? ... I can't carry this nation by myself! … If you're going to treat me like this, please kill me right now; it will be a kindness! Let me out of this impossible situation!'" (Numbers 11:11, 11:13–15 TLB).

Moses felt like he was carrying burdens of over one million people and no one was noticing. We sometimes feel like this, too. We're doing all the work—we're cooking and cleaning after working our day job—and no one's noticing. We become a martyr because we feel like we're doing so much and no one's saying, "Thank you." No one is giving us a medal or a tiara.

Woe is me. My trials are not on display, and I'm not getting sympathy. I'm a martyr.

Favorite phrases of the martyr are:

"No one appreciates me."

"It wouldn't kill anyone to say thank you once in a while."

"Everyone here wouldn't survive without me."

These people are pros at having pity parties. When they are sick or under pressure, they want everybody to know about it.

#3: The Cynic

Solomon was known as the wisest man in the world, yet wisdom and knowledge don't always create happiness. It made Solomon a cynic. He couldn't control where the wisdom and knowledge took his emotions and thinking.

Ecclesiastes says it this way: "'Everything is meaningless'.... What do people get for all their hard work under the sun? ... The earth never changes. ... History merely repeats itself." (Ecclesiastes 1:2–4, 1:9 NLT).

The cynic can see a rainbow in the distance and instead of saying, "Wow, what a beautiful rainbow!" they'll say, "Oh great, more rain." Or, "Look at that rainbow, it's in the shape of a frown."

The cynical outlook sees the worst in everything. As soon as they're born, they're focused on the fact that they're someday going to die. As soon as they're married, they're waiting for the relationship to break apart. A cynic's favorite phrases are: "What's the point? Nothing matters, it isn't going to change anyway."

This habit is a powerful tool in making happy people very, very frustrated and sad.

#4: The Perfectionist

Nothing is ever right or good enough for a perfectionist. God has something to say about this attitude.

Proverbs 27:15 says, "A nagging spouse is like the drip, drip, drip of a leaky faucet" (MSG). You would like some peace, but a perfectionist spouse will nag you to the ends of the earth. This type of complainer is never happy with anything. In the words of Proverbs 21:19, "It's better to live alone in the desert than with a quarrelsome, complaining wife" (NLT).

This applies to husbands as well. He can look to pick fights, point out her imperfections, and be a general clod if he's a perfectionist. This tears a wife down, rips her apart. She's never good enough, never pleasing to him. Would you blame her for thinking about what life would be like without this kind of person?

A perfectionist will always be complaining about something. Take, for example, a newly married fellow who thought he would load the dishwasher. When she noticed how he was loading it, she corrected him, showing him the perfect way. Fine, he thought, she could just do it her way, and he never touched the dishes again. While it's a poor excuse to get out of doing the dishes, it was where his mind went every time she corrected him.

A perfectionist's favorite questions are: "Is that the best you can do? *Is that it?*"

A perfectionist will never say thank you because nothing is good enough. They can never appreciate what is happening around their home or business, because nothing fits their model of perfection. There's a reason why a perfectionist is stuck doing everything.

Three More Kinds of Complainers

#1: Accusers

Accusers blame others and say it's someone else's fault. This problem is their parents' fault, it's society's fault, it's the government's fault, it's the asphalt.

They are always blaming, accusing, but they're never taking responsibility. Look at Adam, who sinned and took it like a man—that is, he blamed his wife. When God called him out on it, he said, "Well, You gave me that woman!" He was an accuser.

#2: Excusers

Excusers say, "I'm a product of my environment. It's not really my fault. It's how I was created. Excuse my bad behavior or my complaining because I got a raw deal. I got the short end of the stick. So, I can be excused for complaining."

The people that are really successful in life are neither accusers nor excusers. These are the people who reach the promised land. They are choosers.

#3: Choosers

Choosers accept responsibility for their own decisions. They choose, in spite of their circumstances, in spite of the pain and difficulty, and in spite of the raw deal they may have gotten, to not complain. In fact, they've chosen to do the opposite. They are positive people.

When everyone else is speaking negatively and speaking down, they speak up. They see the glass as half-full, not half-empty. How do you see the glass in your life?

How to Conquer Complaining

Homes are hotbeds for whining, and nothing destroys the warmth of a home faster than complaining. Nothing destroys the harmony of a marriage faster than whining. Nagging doesn't work; it only makes everyone upset. If your kids are continually complaining, you have to look at yourself and ask if you've set that example. They learned it from somewhere.

How do you conquer complaining? The Bible says, "Do everything without complaining and arguing" (Philippians 2:14 NLT). How do you do that? Is it possible? Yes, but you must apply what you hear. You must put into practice these five things.

#1: Admit complaining is a problem.

If you recognize yourself in any of these categories, admit the problem. You must see that complaining is an issue. Don't just admit it to other people, because if you do, you're simply garnering attention. You're complaining about your complaining problem! Ask them to help keep you accountable to not complain. Most importantly, tell God about it.

Proverbs 28:13 says it like this: "A man who refuses to admit his mistakes can never be successful. But if he confesses and forsakes them, he gets another chance" (TLB).

Often the most difficult part in learning how to handle complaining is recognizing the issue in yourself. If someone recorded you for a week and captured every word that came out of your mouth, what would it reveal about your speech. How much time do you spend griping, complaining, arguing, and saying, "Life stinks"?

Complaining isn't just a bad habit—it's the sin that kept the Israelites out of the promised land. They were assured many great things, including a land that flows with milk and honey, but they wouldn't stop complaining. God was providing miracles in front of their faces, He was answering prayers on the spot, but they were still whining.

Eight times, Scripture says, "they murmured," in passages such as Exodus 16:2 (KJV). Their grumbling culminated when they sent spies into the promised land and were filled with fear and hopelessness—they did not trust that God could fulfill His promise to them. So, they complained:

> That night all the members of the community raised their voices and wept aloud. All the Israelites grumbled against Moses and Aaron, and the whole assembly said to them, "If only we had died in Egypt! Or in this wilderness! Why is the LORD bringing us to this land only to let us fall by the sword? Our wives and children will be taken as plunder. Wouldn't it be better for us to go back to Egypt?" And they said to each other, "We should choose a leader and go back to Egypt."
> **—Numbers 14:1–4** *(NIV)*

This was God's response to their grumbling:

> How long will this wicked community grumble against me? I have heard the complaints of these grumbling Israelites. So tell them, "As surely as I live, declares the LORD, I will do to you the very thing I heard you say: In this wilderness your bodies will fall—every one of you twenty years old or more who was counted in the census and who has grumbled against me. Not one of you will enter the land I swore with uplifted hand to make your home, except Caleb son of Jephunneh and Joshua son of Nun."
> **—Numbers 14:27–30** *(NIV)*

That's how seriously God takes complaining.

You'll never get the life you want or the life you were created for if you complain. You'll never get to your promised land. God can't allow you to enjoy His riches because He won't bless murmuring. He doesn't bless complaining. You simply can never be satisfied.

So, for your own health and well-being, you must stop.

#2: Accept responsibility for your own life.

Complaining is often playing the blame game to get out of your own responsibilities. We put the focus on somebody else to cloud our own failings. Even though I'm the cause of it, maybe if I complain, I can shift the focus and feel a little better.

Proverbs 19:3 says, "People ruin their lives by their own foolishness and then are angry at the LORD" (NLT).

Oftentimes, we do terrible things and suffer the consequences, but then turn around and get mad at God. The children of Israel were angry at God for their own misfortunes, but they could not stop complaining about their circumstances no matter how many times God delivered them. We can't complain about how the ball bounces if we drop it. When I bring problems into my life, I have no legitimate right to complain. The Bible is clear—we reap what we sow (Galatians 6:7). What goes around, comes around.

Some religions have taken that concept and call it karma, but it started with God, who said, "You'll reap what you sow."

Whatever you want in life, you must plant the right seeds. This clear, scriptural principle is summed up in the Golden Rule. If you want friends, you must be friendly. If you want appreciation at home, offer others appreciation.

If you want to be put first in your marriage, you need to put your spouse first in your marriage.

Accept responsibility for your own life and the choices that you make. Choose to change.

#3: Practice being thankful.

Develop the attitude of gratitude. Appreciation is a powerful tool against complaining.

The article about the physical effects of complaining I referred to earlier explained that one way to grow new positive connective neurons in your brain is by having an attitude of gratitude.[15]

First Thessalonians 5:18 says, "Thank God no matter what happens. This is the way God wants you who belong to Christ Jesus to live" (MSG). God says, "I want you to be thankful in all circumstances." He has a pattern in which He designs even the bad things in our lives for good. God's purpose for your life is greater than any problems, so in everything give thanks.

When you develop an attitude of gratitude, no matter your circumstances, you create a tremendous antidote for complaining.

Now, of course there's things in life, marriage, or business that we aren't satisfied with, or some habits in ourselves, our mate, children, or boss, that are frustrating, but there are things in every situation that we can be thankful for. It depends on what we focus on. Is the glass half empty, or half full?

For example, someone at work backstabbed or cheated you. You're not glossing over the bad by saying it's a good thing. You're not saying that you needed to be back-stabbed. The problem is recognizing the good in this situation. Instead of complaining you're getting back-stabbed, you're thankful that someone stepped in to help stop the backstabbing. Someone stuck up for you and told the truth about your character, standing with you instead of against you. Or, that God gave you the ability to withstand the situation. You're recognizing the good in the midst of the bad.

Philippians 4:11 says it like this: "I have learned how to be content with whatever I have" (NLT). When Paul wrote this, he was unjustly imprisoned at Rome. The situations and circumstances Paul went through did not determine his happiness. He teaches us that if he can do it, you can too. Your circumstances do not have to determine your happiness.

When you learn to be happy and joyful in spite of the circumstance, you've reached a new level of maturity. You are not controlled by the circumstances. You are in control of yourself.

Whining about your circumstances and complaining against God means you're saying, "God, you gave me a raw deal. I can't do anything with the circumstances You've handed to me. If I were God, I could do a better job."

Practice an attitude of gratitude and you're telling Him that despite the challenges in your life, you will remain faithful.

#4: Look for God's work in the midst of your circumstances.

You're surrounded by sharks. But, look to see where God is moving and working. You might think He has left you and is a million miles away, but He's working. Good things are happening.

Second Corinthians 4:17–18 (TLB) makes this clear:

> *These troubles and sufferings of ours are, after all, quite small and won't last very long. Yet this short time of distress will result in God's richest blessing upon us forever and ever! So we do not look at what we can see right now, the troubles all around us, but we look forward to the joys in heaven which we have not yet seen. The troubles will soon be over, but the joys to come will last forever.*

Keep a larger perspective. We're here for a short time, while eternity lasts forever. Even in the midst of this short period of suffering that you're going through, God is still moving and working in your life. In eternity, you'll recognize your trials led someone else into heaven because of how you dealt with that circumstance. Who knows? God does. He's working.

A positive life is not the absence of suffering. Bad things happen. Paul is saying problems come into our lives, but the way you look at them determines your attitude. God is working for good in your life, and the wonderful things that you're going to get out of them will be longer lasting than the temporary problem.

Look for God's working in circumstances. Positive

people realize that God is controlling circumstances. He is fitting everything into a pattern, and His purpose is greater than your problem.

By whining, we're sinning. The reason why the Bible tells us not to complain, over and over again, is because it's rebellion against God. When I complain about my circumstances that are beyond my control, I'm telling God that I should be in His seat. That I'm going to look for issues and exploit them to complain about Him.

When you complain, you're challenging God's wisdom. You are wondering if He knows what He's talking about. Does He not see what's going on? Is He really wise?

You're also doubting God's care. It's almost as if you read the story where He counts the very hairs on our head, but then you wonder if He cares about anything other than the fact there may be hair on your head. Does He really see what's going on in your life? Does He love you? You also doubt God's goodness. You forget how good He is and was, and His promise of how good He will be.

Oftentimes, the thing we're complaining about is the aspect that God wants to work in and through us. In other words, there's a situation we don't like and we're struggling and complaining. That should be a sign that God wants to work on an area in you.

For example, you're complaining about your job and that you should get a raise, but God is trying to work on your submission to authority. Maybe He's teaching you how to react when mistreated. Whatever it is, perhaps the issue you're complaining about is where God wants to grow you.

Until we learn the lesson, the issue will keep coming back around. It is a warning light from God, saying, "There's something wrong here. Let's change it. Stop complaining. Start changing!" Listen to Him and look for God's working in the circumstances. You'll learn to be grateful for these powerful lessons.

#5: Speak positively.

Positive speech only works if you speak positively. Jesus is clear when He says in John 13:17, "Now that you know these things, you will be blessed if you do them" (NIV). James 1:22 says to not merely listen to the Word but also do what it says. The blessing doesn't come in the knowledge; it comes in the action. So, when we apply positive speaking, that's when the difference is made.

Positive speaking takes practice. For some people, it isn't easy, but habits are only broken by replacement. You have to swap a new habit in order to overcome an old habit. You have to take your negative complaining and you have to replace it with positive speaking. It's harder than it sounds. It takes practice.

Ephesians 4:29 says, "Don't use foul or abusive language. Let everything you say be good and helpful, so that your words will be an encouragement to those who hear them" (NLT).

Wait a minute—*everything?*

You might say, "Well, I can't tell someone when there's something's wrong?" Instead of pointing out the negative in someone, you can encourage them to do something right.

The Bible says we're going to give an account of every careless word (Matthew 12:36). Paul is saying not to let any junk come out of your mouth, but only words that help people with their needs—that benefit them. If you can't say something good, don't say anything at all. Replace your criticisms and complaints with compliments.

When you visit the gym and the trainer tells you to do ten pushups, and you stare at him. What? Pushups? You try. You're stretching new muscles. It's painful at first, but after keeping with the work, you get better, and you grow muscles. Ten are easier, and you go for fifteen. And soon, you're competing with men and women who have done it their whole lives. It works.

Speaking positively is a crucial factor in parenting. Affirmation gets better results than nagging. Ephesians 6:4 says, "Don't keep on scolding and nagging your children, making them angry and resentful. Rather, bring them up with loving discipline … and godly advice" (TLB). It's not telling you to avoid disciplining your children or overlook their bad behavior. Instead, use loving discipline. Do your words help your kids, or do they hinder your kids? Are you building your kids up or tearing them down? Be positive in your speaking.

Good things happen when you don't complain and instead speak positively. No one can criticize or find fault with positive speech. "It's a beautiful day," you might tell a stranger. "No it's not," they complain in reply. But, they see you differently. Integrity and cleanliness are the result of positive language.

You're a person of integrity, and with integrity comes respect in a dark world—"as children of God, shining like bright lights in a world full of crooked and perverse people" (Philippians 2:15 NLT). Our culture is so negative that when you find a person who is genuinely positive, they shine out like a light in a dark room. People are attracted to positivity like a moth to a flame.

The world is watching the church to see if this Jesus thing is making any difference in our lives. Is it real? Fake? Is there anything to it? When the world is negative and you're being positive, there's an attraction. It opens the door to being able to share the Good News to people. You won't need to force it, it just happens. People ask you because you're such a good witness by your life.

Another reason whining is a problem is because a complaining Christian is a bad witness.

Wouldn't it be great if our churches had the reputation in their communities of "this is where the positive people go"? What if others said of the church, "Those people are always lifting others up, always so encouraging!" Where there is harmony, love, and unity, people will be busting down the doors to get in. Every time you smile, shake somebody's hand, say hi, greet somebody, or give a hug, you are spreading love in this body known as the church. You're making a difference. You're making an impact. You're shining like a star in a dark world.

What would happen in your business if all of the complaining stopped? What would happen in your home if your family made a pact that they wouldn't complain, be critical, or tear each other down?

Here's a challenge—play the complaining money game. It starts with a $5 bet. Whoever complains over the course of a week has to give $5. Carry around cash. Give the kids some money if you need to, a bit of spending money, then explain that anyone who complains has to pay. They might say they'll run out of money. Then, don't complain!

Here's the reality. In order to do this, you need a power beyond yourself, Jesus Christ. He is the antidote to our culture and our nature. He makes us new people inside. Maybe the complaining is an embedded habit. The only way that will be broken, is by an external power in your life who will begin changing you from the inside out.

WORKBOOK

Chapter Four Questions

Question: Describe a person you know who tends toward negativity and complaining. How do you feel after spending time in their presence? Is it easier to see the silliness of their complaints than of your own? Why?

_____

_____

_____

_____

_____

_____

_____

_____

_____

_____

_____

Question: Which of these might sometimes describe you: the whiner, the martyr, the cynic, or the perfectionist? (If you aren't sure and you feel brave, ask your spouse or a close friend!) Give an example from the past week of when you gravitated toward this behavior. Do you try to justify your attitude rather than repenting of it?

_____

_____

_____

_____

_____

_____

_____

_____

_____

_____

_____

Journal: Choose to be a *chooser* rather than an *accuser* or *excuser*. Take time to write down all of your accusations and excuses. Then, tear up that page and write down what you are responsible for, including your decisions and attitudes. Commit to God that you will stop blaming and start trusting Him and being responsible for your own choices.

_____

_____

_____

_____

_____

_____

_____

_____

_____

_____

_____

_____

Action: Start a gratitude list and add to it each day. Use this list in your prayer time. Take ideas from this list and send out a note or text of gratitude to others a few times a week. Look for reasons to thank God even in difficult or frustrating situations, and add these to your list as well.

Chapter Four Notes

_____

_____

_____

_____

_____

_____

_____

_____

_____

_____

_____

_____

_____

_____

_____

_____

_____

_____

_____

_____

_____

CHAPTER FIVE

Stop Biting Others

Sharks can smell blood from a third of a mile away.[16] When they arrive, and there's a lot of blood in the water, they can go into a feeding frenzy. A blind rage comes over them, and they bite like a maniac.[17]

A shark very rarely attacks another shark, and usually only if there is a food dispute.[18] Instead, they swim with focused zeal like armed submarines in the water, waiting to strike. Have you noticed you're not being bitten by sharks? Perhaps that's because *you're* a shark, and you're biting others.

What are the symptoms of someone who bites others? Look inward. Is anger increasing or decreasing in your life? These days, are you more easily angered then you were in the past? Anger can be like a feeding frenzy, blind rage filling you to the point of hurting others.

Think you're immune? When you're cruising the interstate and a Prius has its sights on you and pulls into your lane, almost sideswiping you, then drops below the speed

limit while you're stuck behind them, do you get angry—
or do you let the peace of Christ rule in your heart?

According to a new study by the AAA Foundation for
Traffic Safety, nearly 80 percent of U.S. drivers expressed
significant anger, aggression, or road rage behind the
wheel at least once in the past year.[19] I thought the per-
centage would be higher.

The most alarming findings show that approximately
eight million U.S. drivers engaged in extreme examples
of road rage, including purposefully ramming another vehicle or getting out of the car to confront another driver.
Fascinating.

Many drivers reported engaging in the following types
of road rage:

- Purposefully tailgating (51 percent—over
  half!)
- Yelling at another driver (47 percent)
- Honking to show annoyance or anger (45 per-
  cent)
- Making angry gestures (33 percent—1 in 3!)
- Trying to block another vehicle from changing
  lanes (24 percent)

The research team concluded the study with this statement: "Inconsiderate driving, bad traffic and the daily
stresses of life can transform minor frustrations into dangerous road rage. Far too many drivers are losing
themselves in the heat of the moment and lashing out in

ways that could turn deadly."

Imagine the other aspects of life that might set people off:

- Politics

- Religion

- National issues

- Marriage problems

- Children's behavior

- Parents, in-laws, and other relationship issues

- Long lines

- Coffee shop out of coffee

- Telemarketing robocalls

- Technology issues

- Calories in our favorite foods

- Dogs barking all night

- Favorite team keeps losing

The list could go on.

It seems that most everyone deals with rage. Our society is an angry society.

The problem is that almost no one is teaching how to deal with anger, with the rage that's inside. Whether you're a Christian or not, you need this teaching on anger. It's not *if* you're going to get angry, it's *when*.

Overcoming Your Anger

I have never talked to anyone who's said, "Man, I totally lost my temper and it worked out so well for me." It simply never happens.

Proverbs 14:29 says, "People with understanding control their anger; a hot temper shows great foolishness" (NLT). Notice, it doesn't say people with understanding don't get angry. It just says they know how to control it. So, you need to understand that anger is a God-given emotion. He's wired you in a way to get angry, because sometimes anger is the most appropriate response. For example, when there's an injustice, you should get angry. When someone is hurting the innocent, you should get angry.

If you never get angry, it's a good indication that you don't have much love. Because sometimes the most loving thing to do is to get angry over a bad situation.

But if you're angry over the wrong things, there's a problem. You have to learn how to control your anger and use it wisely. All of us tend to get angry in one of two ways: either we externalize it, or we internalize it. Both of these are inappropriate expressions of anger. Both of them hurt your body and other people.

Let me explain it in a different way. Everyone is either a skunk or a turtle. The person who is the skunk is very external in their anger. They spray it all over the place. Then, everyone around them has that sour face because it just stinks when that happens.

Other people are the turtles. The turtle retreats and hides in his shell. Like, "Oh, I hope it will all just go away." And then there are those who are both. Sometimes you start out as a turtle, until it builds up too much and then you explode out of the shell and you spray all over the place.

Four Keys When Dealing with Anger

#1: Resolve to control it.

Stop saying that you can't control anger, that your temper just happens. You can control it. Everyone can. Stop making excuses.

This is a big deal for me because I'm born Irish. If you're Irish, then you know what that means. The Irish are, stereotypically, either angry or asleep. (Notre Dame's athletic teams are called the Fighting Irish for a reason!) Before I had the peace of Christ in my life, I was running hot all the time. Always biting, in a feeding frenzy.

When Christ came into my life, He changed everything. I'm not perfect, but I learned how to deal with anger in better ways. Proverbs 29:11 says, "Fools give full vent to their rage, but the wise bring calm in the end" (NIV). We are to demonstrate calm rather than rage.

Anger is a choice. When you tell someone that they make you mad, do they *have* to make you mad? You're choosing to let them make you mad. Sometimes people say they can't help themselves, they just naturally get riled. You can control your anger far more than you think you can, if you're properly motivated.

Have you ever been driving and you're furious at the slow vehicles in front of you? Everyone is Sunday driving every day of the week, and you have places to be and things to do, so you're weaving in and out of traffic and you're making speed happen. You're racing down the freeway and giving people the business as you drive by— but then, all of a sudden, you see a cop. You slow down and wave. "Go blue! Thank you for what you do!"

All of a sudden, you're calm, and you've slowed down. What happened? You were properly motivated. Suddenly, you're not at all angry.

Here's the secret: you have to decide in advance that you *can* control your anger. Don't wait to decide when your temperature has reached a boiling point and your muscles are tense. No, that's too late. Choose in advance that you're going to work on your rising anger and slow your temper.

Have you ever said to yourself, "If that person says that one more time, I'm going to blow a gasket"? What do you do? As soon as they say it, you jump all over them.

How about taking the opposite approach and saying, "If that person says that, I'm going to respond calmly"? In advance, you're saying that the situation won't get to you. You can do the same in every setting, even traffic.

#2: Remember the cost of anger.

You're less likely to get angry if you realize that there's always a cost that comes with your anger. It costs something every single time you lose your temper.

The Bible is clear about the price of uncontrolled anger. Proverbs 14:29 says, "A quick-tempered person stockpiles stupidity" (MSG).

There's a price to pay for angry outbursts. "Anger causes mistakes"(Proverbs 14:29 TLB), and "hot tempers start fights" (Proverbs 15:18 MSG). And, "a hot-tempered man ... gets into all kinds of trouble" (Proverbs 29:22 TLB). In your experience, do you know those sayings to be true? I'm sure we both could share some amusing stories about what people have done when they've gotten angry and the consequences that have resulted.

The *Arizona Republic* reported that Steve Tran was fed up with the cockroach problem in his apartment.[20] After his landlord ignored his requests for help, he decided to take matters into his own hands. He bought twenty-five bug bombs, activated them, and then closed the door on the activated bug bombs. He thought he would see the last of the cockroaches that shared his apartment.

According to the label, just two canisters of the fumigant would have easily solved Tran's roach problem. Even one would have solved the problem. Twenty-five is way too many.

When the spray reached the pilot light of the stove, it ignited, blasting his screen door across the street, breaking all his windows, melting his carpet, and setting his furniture on fire. He said, "I really wanted to kill all of them. ... I thought if I use a lot more, it lasts me longer."

The blast caused over $10,000 of damage to his apartment building. As Proverbs 29:11 says, "only a fool gives full vent to his anger" (paraphrase).

You always lose when you lose your temper. You lose the respect of others and the love is tested of people you love most. You may lose your job due to an uncontrolled temper. Certainly, if you mishandle anger, you can lose your health. You always lose when you lose your temper.

Proverbs 11:29 says it like this: "The fool who provokes his family to anger and resentment will finally have nothing worthwhile left" (TLB).

Let's turn this around. When a person gets angry with you, does that draw you closer to them or push you away from them? It always pushes you further away. You don't feel close to people who are angry with you. You feel far away. You feel distant and if you are angry at your kids all the time, you are pushing them away from you. Even if you show love at other times, you are driving your children away from you.

Understand this, too: in your family and with others, anger is contagious. If you are angry at home all the time, guess what? Your kids are picking up on how to react to situations like you do.

A national study on how kids view their parent's stress and anger is revealing—second-hand stress is a big problem for kids.[21] In a recent survey, researchers interviewed more than one thousand children in grades 3 to 12 and asked them, "If you were granted one wish to change the way your mother's/father's work affects your life, what would that wish be?" Kids' answers were striking.

They rarely wished for extra face time with their parents. Instead, they wished that their parents would be less stressed out and tired. But, the parents in the survey were completely out of touch. None of them guessed that their kids would use their one wish to reduce their stress.

Researchers then asked the children to grade their parents on an anger management scale. More than 40 percent of kids gave their moms and dads a C, D, or F for "controlling his/her temper when I do something that makes him/her angry."

Anger is contagious and concerning. You learned it somewhere, and you're modeling it for your kids. It rubs off on others. If you are around angry people, you will tend to become an angry person. If children grow up in a home full of anger, they learn to be angry. Proverbs 22:24 says, "Don't ... associate with hot-tempered people or you will learn to be like them" (NLT).

It's not simply an issue within a family, either. Dating a man or woman who has an anger issue is a sign you should break up with them. Don't hang around. You're just asking for trouble. You can love the person, but it doesn't mean you should marry them. You ought to wait until they get this area of their life under control. There's help for them. There's counseling. Do you think marriage is going to suddenly change the person? Only a desire to change and the help of Christ can change a person for the better.

Nobody's perfect, but I'm not talking about perfection here. Yet, the Bible is clear. Stop the pattern of anger. Resolve to control your anger. Remember the cost if you don't.

#3: Reflect before you react.

Take a moment before you act. In other words, think before you speak. Don't respond impulsively. Get your mind in gear before you put your mouth in motion. The clichés go on, but there are many because getting a grip on your anger is important.

This is important because anger control is largely a matter of mouth control. If you can watch your words, if you can manage your mouth, if you can control your tongue, you're going to control your temper. They go together.

One translation of Proverbs 29:11 says, "A stupid man gives free rein to his anger; a wise man waits and lets it grow cool" (NEB). There is a biblical precedent, right there, for the term "chill out!"

Have you noticed you can't put your foot in your mouth when your lips are closed? The problem is, we like to speak. And, if we speak enough, we're inevitably going to say something wrong, something hurtful, something selfish, or something dumb. Perhaps all of those things at once. According to studies, the average person speaks more than fifteen thousand words a day.[22] You're bound to say something wrong in all of that.

The point is, delay is a great remedy for anger. The wise man waits and lets his rage cool. Reflect before reacting. The longer you pause your temper, the more it improves. You give yourself time to reflect, time to think, time to step back.

There have been many times in arguments, sometimes with my wife, when one of us in the conflict would say, "Hang on a minute. We need to just cool down a minute." There's nothing wrong with that. Sometimes you just need to take a step back for a minute, or two minutes—or longer.

The Bible tells us to deal with our anger but to do it in a calm way. Taking a step back often makes you realize that it isn't a big deal. You can overlook the situation and don't need to let it internalize. You don't need to punch your fist through the wall to cool off.

"A wise man restrains his anger and overlooks insults. This is to his credit" (Proverbs 19:11 TLB). Take a moment and reflect before acting.

#4: Release anger appropriately.

Is it possible to be angry and not sin? Ephesians 4:26 says, "If you are angry, don't sin by nursing your grudge" (TLB). Notice from this verse that it is possible to be angry yet not sin. Anger is not a sin. It's what you do with the anger that makes it either appropriate or inappropriate—sinful or not.

There is a right way to get angry and a wrong way to get angry. There's a helpful or harmful way to express wrath. You need to learn to release anger appropriately. Jesus, for example, clearly got angry in Scripture—He made a whip and kicked people out of the Temple (church) for using people's love of God to make money unfairly off of them. (John 2:12–25).

God says this is the appropriate kind of anger. It's righteous anger. It wasn't selfish anger; instead, it was righteousness. However, if you're getting angry to get even, that's the wrong kind of fury.

Romans 12:17–21 tells us about some inappropriate ways to release anger: "Never pay back evil with more evil. ... Dear friends, never take revenge. Leave that to the righteous anger of God. ... Don't let evil conquer you, but conquer evil by doing good" (NLT). Releasing your anger appropriately isn't wrong. In fact, as we saw, it does good.

Suppression Versus Repression

What is the appropriate way to express anger? Don't suppress it. Don't store it up inside. If you don't talk it out, you're going to take it out in the wrong ways. Anytime you press anger down inside of you, you're hurting yourself. Cooling off and talking it out calms down the volcano rising inside.

Some of you are stuffers. When you stuff anger inside continually, you are suppressing your anger, in which case, Job 18:4 says, "You're only hurting yourself with your anger" (GNT). It's going to take itself out in all kinds of physical and emotional ailments.

What's the difference between suppression and repression? Repression is total denial, denying that you're angry when you are burning with rage inside. Sometimes Christians particularly fall for this one: because we think we shouldn't be angry, we just repress it. We deny that we're angry. Have you noticed this? Someone says, "You're getting angry." I'm not angry. "I can tell you're angry." I am not angry!

There is a word for repressed anger: depression. Depression is often repressed anger. You've internalized it. You've pushed it down. You've denied it. You haven't dealt with it. Depression is sometimes called frozen rage. It's locked inside and allowed to turn to compost, where depression allows other problems to grow.

Some of you have been depressed for years. What is it

that you're pretending isn't a problem in your life? Your marriage, your job, your kids? You're not going to get any better at controlling the anger, and the depression is not going to leave, until you bring your problems out in the light and get help. Get with somebody, talk it out, deal with it and resolve the problem and get on with your life and be happy again. But, it's your choice. No one is going to make you.

So, what do you do? The next point for keeping your cool is the solution for long-term change. If you want to break a lifetime habit or pattern of anger, you must become a new person.

Renew Your Mind

We have discussed complaining and the brain, how science has shown that connections are made when we complain so it is easier to complain the next time and the next time. A pattern grows. This is how anger works as well. As we get angry in situations and we continuously respond in the same way, brain patterns connect and grow stronger until we react angrily to nearly everything. It becomes our natural response.

How do we break this pattern? Change the way you think. Romans 12:2 says to "be transformed by the renewing of your mind" (NIV). Renew your mind with good thoughts, with gratitude, with praise, and renew your brain in a positive way.

The way you act is determined by the way you feel, and the way that you feel is determined by the way you think. If you want to change the way you feel and the way you act, you must change the way you think.

To change the way you think, you'll need to do some mental reconditioning. You're going to have to fill your mind with the Word of God, and you're going to have to memorize verses so that God can bring them to mind when the anger starts to boil up.

Since anger is learned, the good news is, like worry, it can be unlearned. You don't have to stay stuck in those lousy patterns of anger. You can change. You can learn new patterns with God's help.

But here's the twist: you're not going to get better on your own. You've tried, and you can't. There's no way you can change a lifelong pattern of inappropriate anger just by saying, "I'm going to do it!" You must rely on God's help.

Colossians 3:15 says, "Let the peace of Christ rule in your hearts" (NIV). His peace is the secret. God's power to change is when you get the peace of Christ in your heart to replace the anger in your heart. Your relationship with Christ will determine how patient you are in life.

I played professional baseball, and one season, halfway through my professional baseball career, I accepted Christ into my life. Now remember, I said that I was an angry Irishman, and you can imagine I'd caused some fights and brawls on the baseball field when calls didn't go my way, or when the batter stared at a long fly ball that went so far it should have had a flight attendant on it. But, when I accepted Christ, He made a change in my life and heart.

It was one of my teammates who noticed the change in me. This was confirmation that Christ's peace was ruling in my heart. He could recall rough reactions I'd had to various situations in the past, but suddenly, he saw that I was reacting differently. After a while, he finally asked the question: "What is up with you this season?"

I asked him what he meant, and he said I was just different and calmer. "Did you grow up?"

It was a great opportunity to share with him that I accepted Jesus Christ as my Lord and Savior. I knew that I couldn't do it on my own anymore. I was angry at everything, but then I gave my life over to Christ. I'm not perfect, but He's made a difference. Peace started ruling in my heart instead of my anger. All of a sudden, in situations that usually tripped me up, I could react differently and see them from a different perspective. This time, a godly perspective.

He'll do the same thing for you if you let Him rule your heart. If you have a close relationship with Christ and He carries His power into every area of your life, then you will be a very patient person. If you have a casual relationship with Christ—if you are a fringe Christian and Christ is in your life, but He only has part of your life—then all the other parts of you are left open to anger, impatience, and other sharks. Or, you might become the shark for others.

The more God controls your life, the more patient you're going to become. How does He help me manage my anger? He does it by dealing with the root issues of frustration, fear, and hurt. Jesus says in Matthew 12:34, "Whatever is in your heart determines what you say" (NLT). The Bible teaches that the heart of the problem is a problem of the heart. The problem is not my mouth, which is a symptom of the problem; the true issue lies in my heart. Because whatever comes out of the mouth is what's in the heart.

What you really need in anger management is a heart transplant. You need a new heart. And, I know where you can get one. His name is Jesus Christ, and He specializes in heart transplants. And, all the therapy and all the self-help books and podcasts in the world cannot give you a new heart. Only Jesus Christ can do that.

The Bible says when anyone becomes a new Christian, you become a new person inside and you get a new heart (2 Corinthians 5:17). The old has passed away; the new has come. David says in Psalm 51:10, "Create in me a pure heart, O God" (NIV). That's what you need to pray.

Jesus Christ can deal with the root issues of your anger. He can replace your frustrated heart with one filled with love. He's in control and you're not. But, when you place Him in control of your life, then you have a peace that goes beyond all human understanding (Philippians 4:7). You're not swimming through the oceans, looking for blood.

And it's not just anger God helps. He can replace your hurting heart with His love. You may have been rejected as a child or as an adult. You may have been abandoned. You may have been abused. You may have felt unloved. And, you may have felt lonely. Yet, Christ is with you. He's there.

God sees your pain, and no one in the whole world cares more about it than Jesus Christ. Your pain matters to God, and you matter to God. He can replace the hurt in your heart, the struggles that you've been denying and pushing down, and with genuine love, you will find your anger diminishing. Jesus can replace your insecurities, fears, and anxieties with His peace and His power.

Why don't you say, "Jesus Christ, come into my life and replace all the ugliness in my heart with all the goodness that You have?"

Chapter Five Questions

Question: What are some "triggers" that cause you to feel anger or rage? Do you tend to express your anger externally or stuff it inwardly? What price have you paid for your unrighteous anger, both in your own life and in your relationships with others?

_____

_____

_____

_____

_____

_____

_____

_____

_____

Question: What are some practical ways you can step back and cool down instead of reacting in the heat of your anger? What are some healthy and appropriate ways to express and release anger?

_____

_____

_____

_____

_____

_____

_____

_____

_____

_____

_____

Journal: Examine the root issues and wrong thought patterns that lead to your anger. Ask God for understanding and to show you the right thinking, based on His Word, that will set you free. Commit to taking control of your anger in the power of Christ.

_____

_____

_____

_____

_____

_____

_____

_____

_____

_____

_____

_____

Action: Talk to a mentor or mature Christian friend about your particular struggles with anger. Come up with a plan together to help you build healthy habits of response to anger-inducing situations. Ask your friend to keep you accountable and encourage you as you obey God in making the changes He is calling—and enabling—you to make.

Chapter Five Notes

CHAPTER SIX

Don't Feed the Sharks!

Every day, people jump in the ocean. And every day, most of those people don't see a shark.

Because the ocean is big, you could say that by swimming in the ocean, you're technically swimming with the sharks. In that light, you could similarly say that because you're jogging along the streets of San Diego, you're running with bears, since somewhere on land, they're roaming, looking for food. It's improbable, yet possible.

Change the odds a bit. Let loose a bear on the streets of San Diego. Cover yourself in honey. Then, run. The odds go up a bit that you will see a bear.

On a beach, lifeguards watch for sharks. If they are spotted, signs are posted that a shark has been seen in the area, and to swim at your own risk. Can you imagine what would happen if a lifeguard or a swimmer who spotted a shark tossed chopped up fish into the water? Feeding frenzy.

Why feed the sharks?

The world creates feeding frenzies. Advertisers know that everybody's interested in change. So, ads on how to get better are going to get our attention. Did you know that in recent years, self-help books have pulled in over $10 billion?[23] And the market is growing. We're always looking for the latest tip, the latest hot idea, the latest therapy, fad, or whatever will instantly change our lives for the better.

The fact is, all of us have areas of our lives that we wish we could change. What do you have a hard time controlling? Your temper? Sexual desires? Drinking? Spending? Eating? Moods? Procrastination? Bad habits? Whatever it might be, we're eager to get control.

These are areas we wish we could change, but we have been unable to. The question this chapter will answer is, "Why do I do what I don't want to do?" That's an old question, and Paul mentions it in the book of Romans.

The Apostle Paul could easily be considered the greatest Christian ever to live. Yet, in this section of Scripture, we get to see through a window into his soul and get a glimpse of the fact that this giant of the Christian faith struggled like we do. The entire passage reads like a poet's cry to God:

> *I do not understand what I do. For what I want to do I do not do, but what I hate I do. And if I do what I do not want to do, I agree that the law is good. As it is, it is no longer I myself who do it, but it is sin living in me. For I know that good itself does not dwell in me, that is, in my sinful nature. For I have the desire to do what is good, but I cannot carry it out. For I do not do the good I want to do, but the evil I do not want to do—this I keep on doing. Now if I do what I do not want to do, it is no longer I who do it, but it is sin*

living in me that does it. So I find this law at work: Alt-hough I want to do good, evil is right there with me. For in my inner being I delight in God's law; but I see another law at work in me, waging war against the law of my mind and making me a prisoner of the law of sin at work within me. What a wretched man I am! Who will rescue me from this body that is subject to death? Thanks be to God, who deliv-ers me through Jesus Christ our Lord!
—Romans 7:15–25 (NIV)

It's freeing to know there's a victory you can claim. This victory, as Paul says, is through Christ, who can deliver us from this dilemma.

The Problem: Sin Nature

Why is it that I do what I don't want to do? Why do I have such a hard time getting my act together and getting things under control?

The Bible says it simply: we struggle because of our sinful nature. What is a sinful nature? It just means that you and I have a natural predisposition to do the wrong thing.

Paul's personal example, above, seems something that every person deals with: "I do not understand what I do. For what I want to do I do not do, but what I hate I do" (Romans 7:15 NIV). There's a civil war inside all of us. Jesus discussed this, too, when He said, "The spirit is will-ing, but the flesh is weak" (Matthew 26:41 NIV).

We have a willingness for good, but carrying it out is difficult. Even after you become a believer, there is ten-sion inside of you. Some pastors and theologians have

argued that Paul is talking about the tension before he became a Christian, but this is why it's important to know
your Greek—because if he were only discussing his old
self, Paul would have been speaking in the aorist tense,
which is the past tense in Greek.

Instead, Paul uses the present tense Greek verb to describe his struggle, so we know Paul is struggling with the
things you and I struggle with, even though we are Christians. You have your good nature, which God has given
you, but you also have your old sinful nature that is pulling at you until heaven.

Have you ever tried to break a bad habit? It works well
for a couple of weeks. But, it is a matter of time before
you're back to what you used to do all along. You say,
"I'd like to change but I just can't. I feel like Paul here."
We've all been there.

Good intentions are never good enough. Good resolutions aren't going to make you choose goodness. It takes
more than simply the desire to change. Since everybody
deals with the sin struggle and the civil war that's inside
of us, the results are pretty predictable. At times, we will
fail. Yet, with God's help, we succeed.

Paul's Prediction:
Three Results of the Struggle

Sometimes, though, the struggle can leave us confused,
frustrated, and discouraged. Let's look at each one in detail so we can get a better idea how to overcome each one.

#1: Confusion

We often have confusion in our lives because of the tension between wanting to do what's right and ending up not doing it. You wonder why you're not overcoming sin, why it's just not happening for you, and why are you still struggling with this stuff.

Look again at Romans 7:15: "I do not understand what I do. For what I want to do I do not do, but what I hate I do" (NIV). Have you ever wondered why you act in ways that don't make sense, even to yourself? Have you ever wondered, "Why do I keep making the same mistake over and over? I don't understand myself." There's confusion in your life because of the old nature.

#2: Frustration

Frustration is the natural byproduct of this civil war inside of you. This is why a lot of people give up on the faith because they think that Christianity is an instant freedom from all sin issues.

Paul says in Romans 7:18, "I have the desire to do what is good, but I cannot carry it out" (NIV). How many times have you started each week or each morning with great intentions? Today's going to be different! But by evening, or by the end of the week, nothing has really changed.

How many diets have started in the morning and by the end of the day you're in for a balanced meal, a hamburger in each hand? It's frustrating. You want to change but you just can't. You have the motivation but not the determination. You can't pull it off. You have the desire to do good, but you don't have the power.

This is the problem with every self-help book. Self-help books often have very good advice in them, but they don't give you the power to make the change. Technically, there should only be one self-help book, because after you read it, you've helped yourself and you need nothing else.

Change is hard.

This leads to the third result of the civil war inside of you.

#3: Discouragement

Hear the discouraged tone in Paul's voice in a para-phrase of Romans 7:24: "I've tried everything and nothing helps. I'm at the end of my rope. Is there no one who can do anything for me?" (MSG).

Do you hear his discouragement in here? *"I've lost the battle. I'm ready to give up. My life's a mess. I'm a failure. Why even try? Why not just throw in the towel and get used to living life as a failure? I'll never be able to change."*

All of us have felt that frustration of the civil war inside of us—the good and the bad in a tug of war. You're confused and frustrated, and it leads to discouragement. You are stuck in the cycle of good intentions. Then failure. Then guilt. Then action, then good intentions, then failure again. It's like being on a hamster wheel that goes around and round. You're putting out energy and effort with no permanent progress.

We understand that the struggle with our flesh and the reality of life is our sin nature. It's why you're not perfect and won't be until you get to heaven.

But until then, we fight the old nature inside of us.

If you've ever felt this way, I've got some good news for you: there is a way out.

Personal Freedom

We are free. Free to fail, free to succeed. What is this freedom? Is it freedom to fail? The old nature says we are going to fail every time. Yet, with Christ, we can find freedom to succeed.

In John 8:32 Jesus says, "You will know the truth, and the truth will set you free" (NIV). God has promised that we can be free from this circling trap. The secret to personal change is not willpower, not a pill, nor is it a resolution or vow. In fact, it's nothing you can do or say. The secret to personal change is something you know. You know the truth.

When you change the way you think, it changes the way you feel. And, when you change the way you feel, it changes the way you act.

To change the way you think, you must look at what you believe. Behind every self-defeating act is a lie you're believing.

For example, pretend you're accepting an idea that just isn't true. It is a lie about yourself, such as, "I'm useless." It's a lie that came about because of your past, something someone said about you. It includes a lie about God's goodness—that He wouldn't create trash, you tell yourself, "except me." You listen and believe those lies, and it holds you back, keeps you down. You feel terrible about yourself.

In truth, you're a gift from God, carefully designed and planned to the minutest detail to serve and worship Him, and then so loved by Christ that He died for you. If you believe He loves you, then your thinking changes along with your actions.

Yet, we choose to believe otherwise. Why do you do something that you know is bad for you? Because there is some kind of a payoff. What's the payoff? "This will make me feel good." Or, "I deserve this." Or, "It's okay, this is my 'thing.'"

When you know the truth, the truth will set you free. What you must do is uncover and expose the lies you've been accepting.

If you're going to change, you're going to have to face the truth. I'm going to ask you to face the truth about yourself. And, I'm going to ask you to face the truth about God and about your problems.

How do you face the truth? The Bible gives us four things to do. These things are simple for me to share with you, but they can be difficult to do.

The Prescription

#1: Acknowledge the root of your problem.

Most of us go through life with this vague feeling that something is wrong with my life but can't put a finger on it. You know something's out of whack, out of kilter, but you simply can't figure it out. But, God can figure it out, and He tells us. He has a word for the problem. In today's culture, it's not a popular word: sin.

What is sin? Sin is not a behavior. Sin starts in the mind. Sin produces sinful behavior.

Sin is ignoring God. It's saying, "I'm not going to listen to You, God. I'm going to do what I want to do, what I think is right. I'm going to play god. I'm god and You're not."

When you spell "sin," what's the middle letter? "I"— that's the problem. I am the problem. I think that I know better than God. We think we know better about what will make us happy. What makes it worse is that we live in a state of perpetual denial about our sinfulness. We all deal with it, and to deny it is to worsen the civil war inside you. First John 1:8 says, "If we claim to be without sin, we deceive ourselves and the truth is not in us" (NIV).

- *Principle of life:* Sin always involves self-deception.
- *Fact of life:* To stop defeating myself, I must stop deceiving myself.

Come to grips with the reality of the situation. You must take an honest look at your life and face the truth to deal with the issues. What are you pretending isn't a problem? What addiction are you pretending you don't fight? Because all sin is addictive in some form. What is it in your life that you're saying, "It's no big deal!" If sin is the sickness, you cannot get well until you stop denying and deceiving yourself.

Sadly, too often we don't change until we hit bottom.

And, things have to get really, really bad. That's unfortunate because it's not necessary. You don't have to go that far down. You can acknowledge the root of the issue and deal with sin.

It's a common saying in counseling studies that people wait too long to get help. While you're never too far gone for God to help, sometimes it makes it difficult. After a while, it's almost impossible to turn around an issue that is embedded inside and is affecting people. A marriage will be carrying on, with warning signs all over the place that there's a problem. Then, all of a sudden, the husband or the wife walks out. And, now there's a wake-up call for the spouse left behind.

They come to the counselor and say, "What can I do now?" Not a whole lot. You should have been working on it a whole lot sooner. Most people wait until it's too late and go through pain that's unnecessary.

Why? Because they were living in denial.

#2: Believe that Jesus can change you.

If you want to keep sharks from biting, acknowledge the truth about yourself and then believe that Christ can change you. Let's go back to the question Paul asked and notice his answer in the next verse. Romans 7:24–25 says, "Who will free me from this life that is dominated by sin and death? Thank God! The answer is in Jesus Christ our Lord" (NLT).

The answer to your problem is a person. Who is going to be lord of your life? Who will call the shots? You or Jesus Christ? Paul says Jesus can set you free. When you

SHARK WEAK · 129

are mastered by Him, you can master your problems. God has the power you were lacking. He'll help you out.

Jesus Christ knows what we are going through. He came to earth to be tempted, just as we are, to deal with our personal sharks and vices. He overcame them. He suffered death, torture, tragedy, and heartache. So, as we call on Him, He will climb down to the hole you're in, get into the mud with you, then lift and pull you out. He knows what you're going through.

That's exactly what Paul says in Romans 8:2: "For the power of the life-giving Spirit—and this power is mine through Christ Jesus—has freed me from the vicious circle of life and death" (TLB).

We go through a vicious cycle. Good intentions, failure, guilt, good intentions, failure, guilt. How are you going to break out of it? It's not listening to another self-help podcast or reading another self-help book. Those might offer short term solutions and positive habits and thinking, yet ultimately they will fail. It's getting the power of Jesus Christ into your life. Acknowledging the problem and then believe that Christ can change me will break the cycle.

#3: Confess the struggle to another person.

Talking about your struggles with a fellow believer is a biblical principle of recovery. This is an absolute prerequisite to healing and wholeness from God, and there are many reasons why it is essential. Yet, this is the hardest part for a lot of people. You say you can acknowledge your issues—I believe that Jesus will make the difference—but wait, I need to confess to another person?

Yes. Here's God's command: "Confess your sins to each other and pray for each other so that you may be healed. The earnest prayer of a righteous person has great power and produces wonderful results" (James 5:16 NLT).

When a believing person prays, your world changes for the better. You need other people praying for you.

You also need accountability. Why? Because ego prevents healing. "I don't want anybody to find out about my problem!" Yet, they will know, even if you don't tell them. It's pride that is holding you back, and your pride is a shark that swims toward others, threatening to bite them and keeping them from helping you. God has wired us in a way that we need each other. Relationships. That's what the church is for. A safe place to create relationships built on Christ.

Church is the place for people who've admitted, "I have an old sin nature and I have a war going on in my life that's constant. I'm on my way. I'm working on it. But, I believe that Jesus Christ can make a difference in my life. I'm willing to humble myself, and I'm willing to admit when I've blown it and need help and accountability. I want to get better. I want to live by the Spirit."

There's no room in church for perfection or a show. It's a place to be real and honest. I'm more interested in getting it together than in pretending I've got it all together. Sometimes I'll hear people who don't go to church say the reason they don't go to church is because "the church is full of hypocrites." And we like to say, "And there is always room for one more!"

You're welcome at Skyline Church unless you have it all together. If you're perfect, you don't need church. Because at our church, "No Perfect People Allowed" is one of our slogans. We don't have it all together, and we're willing to admit it as we learn and grow to become better people in Jesus Christ.

#4: Dedicate yourself to Jesus.

Surrender entirely to Christ. You need a power that is greater than yourself. Romans 6:12–13 says, "Do not let sin control the way you live…. Instead, give yourselves completely to God, for you were dead but now you have new life" (NLT).

Every day you are controlled by something whether you like it or not. You may be controlled by your own ego, expectations of other people, fear, resentment or bitterness against somebody else, guilt, a substance, or a habit.

> *The temptations in your life are no different from what others experience. And God is faithful. He will not allow the temptation to be more than you can stand. When you are tempted, he will show you a way out so that you can endure.*
> **—1 Corinthians 10:13** (GW)

Freedom comes when you choose what's going to control you. When you choose Jesus Christ to be the controlling factor in your life—when I am mastered by the Master—I can master everything else. If God is not number one in your life, something else will control you. You choose.

What area of your life haven't you given over to Jesus Christ totally? For some, it's having more faith. For others, it's giving, or it's anger. What happens when God has every bit of your life? The theological term for giving over every part of my life is sanctification. I'm handing over more and more of my life to Jesus Christ. What areas are you holding back?

What happens when you take this step and dedicate your life fully?

How do we begin to make this change?

Making the Change

There's something real about coming to Christ and saying, "I'm going to give You everything in my life." Why not give it all to Christ? What have you got to lose? The only thing you'll miss is a sense that you have some control.

If you just stop in chapter 7, it can be a little discouraging, but right after Romans 7 is one of my favorite chapters in all of Scripture. In Romans 8, Paul explains the result of his own struggles and his realization of what it actually means to live the Christian life, even if it's a struggle sometimes.

There are two parts to it. One is justification, that I am made right with God. That's what God has done—He did that, not you. You believed, and you were made right. Where you really come in is in the sanctification part.

So now there is no condemnation for those who belong to Christ Jesus [even though you and I struggle, we are not condemned, because we've been justified]. And because you belong to him, the power of the life-giving Spirit has freed you from the power of sin that leads to death.
—Romans 8:1–2 *(NLT)*

Now you're free, so walk in that freedom. Don't return to the mess you left. Take the path of discipleship and follow Jesus. It's a process, so you grow closer and closer as you walk toward Him. That's sanctification. I'm setting my feet in Jesus' direction, not toward my sinful nature and flesh.

God hasn't taken away our free will. We choose what we want to get closer to every day. Do you want to walk down the path toward Jesus or further away? It's your choice. He justified you. What are you going to do with it?

The law of Moses was unable to save us, because of the weakness of our sinful nature. So, God did what the law could not do. He sent his own Son in human form, like the bodies we sinners have. And, in that body, God declared an end to sin's control over us, by giving his Son as a sacrifice for our sins. He did this so that the just requirement of the law would be fully satisfied for us, who no longer follow our sinful nature but instead follow the Spirit.

Those who are dominated by the sinful nature think about sinful things, but those who are controlled by the Holy Spirit think about things that please the Spirit. So letting your sinful nature control your mind leads to death.
—Romans 8:5–6 *(NLT)*

Remember, what you think affects how you feel, and how you feel affects how you act or behave. Paul makes special mention that it's not your body you must control, but your mind. Because everything starts there.

Then the chapter goes on to talk about the key to finding victory. This is how you overcome:

> But letting the Spirit control your mind leads to life and peace. For the sinful nature is always hostile to God. It never did obey God's laws, and it never will. That's why those who are still under the control of their sinful nature can never please God. But you are not controlled by your sinful nature. You are controlled by the Spirit if you have the Spirit of God living in you. (And remember that those who do not have the Spirit of Christ living in them do not belong to him at all.) And Christ lives within you, so even though your body will die because of sin, the Spirit gives you life because you have been made right with God. The Spirit of God, who raised Jesus from the dead, lives in you. And just as God raised Christ Jesus from the dead, he will give life to your mortal bodies by this same Spirit living within you. Therefore, dear brothers and sisters, you have no obligation to do what your sinful nature urges you to do. For if you live by its dictates, you will die. But if through the power of the Spirit you put to death the deeds of your sinful nature, you will live. For all who are led by the Spirit of God are children of God.
> —**Romans 8:6b–14** (NLT)

Paul says the key is dedicating your all to Christ is sanctification. When it's our choice who or what controls us, we have to surrender every day if we want victory over our issues. He's not saying that those who are Christians won't sin, but there's a difference in stumbling on the path toward Jesus and not being on the path at all. Being on the path matters to God.

This is why Paul answers his question in Romans 7:24, "Who will free me from this life that is dominated by sin and death?" in the following verse by saying, "Thank God! The answer is in Jesus Christ our Lord" (NLT).

There was a writer and theologian named Henri Nouwen who became fascinated with a group of trapeze artists called the Flying Rodleighs. There was something about their courage, their trusting and dependence on each other, that inspired him. He felt that it was a parable of life with God.

One day, he said, "I was sitting with Rodleigh, the leader of the troupe, talking about flying."[24] And Rodleigh explained:

"As a flyer, I must have complete trust in my catcher. The public might think that I'm the great star of the trapeze, but the real star is Joe, my catcher. He has to be there with split second precision and grab me out of the air as I come to him out of the air."

"How does it work?" I asked.

"The secret," he said, "is that the flyer does nothing and the catcher does everything. When I fly to Joe, I have simply to stretch out my arms and hands and wait for him to catch me and pull me safely over the apron behind the catch bar."

"You do nothing?" I said, surprised.

"Nothing," Rodleigh repeated. "The worst thing the flyer can do is try to catch the catcher. I'm not supposed to catch Joe. It's Joe's task to catch me. I simply put my arms out in surrender. If I grab Joe's wrists, I might break them, or he might break mine and that would be the end for both of us. A flyer must fly and a catcher must catch

and the flyer must trust with outstretched arms that his
catcher will be there for him."

Our part is to trust and surrender every day to Jesus.
God's part is to catch. To hold. To do in me what I can't
do for myself. Fly to Him, arms out. He'll catch you.

Stop trying. Start trusting. Remember 2 Corinthians
5:17: "This means that anyone who belongs to Christ has
become a new person. The old life is gone; a new life has
begun!" (NLT). He'll give you that new power to overcome anything keeping you down.

WORKBOOK

Chapter Six Questions

Question: What are some bad habits you have (or some good habits you fail to enact)? Have you made resolutions in these areas and still fallen short? How has this led to confusion, frustration, and discouragement in your life?

_____

_____

_____

_____

_____

_____

_____

_____

_____

_____

Question: What are some ways *sin* is hidden, rationalized, diagnosed, or reasoned away in today's culture? What effect does this sin-denying mindset have on people receiving the gospel and putting their faith in Jesus Christ? Have you adopted the world's beliefs when facing the struggles of your own sinful nature? How can you be honest with yourself and God about the true nature of your problems?

_____

_____

_____

_____

_____

_____

_____

_____

_____

_____

_____

Journal: *Behind every self-defeating act is a lie I'm believing.* Look back at your list of bad habits from the first question. Trace each one to the lie that fuels your thinking and feelings. What does God's Word say?

_____

_____

_____

_____

_____

_____

_____

_____

_____

_____

_____

_____

_____

Action: Read Luke 9:23. Do you begin each day consciously choosing to trust Jesus completely and surrender fully to Him? Write out a short prayer of dedication with which to start each day.

_____

_____

_____

_____

_____

_____

_____

_____

Chapter Six Notes

_____

_____

_____

_____

_____

_____

_____

_____

_____

_____

_____

_____

_____

_____

_____

_____

_____

_____

_____

_____

_____

_____

_____

CHAPTER SEVEN

Take the Bite Out of Your Words

People love to talk.

Talk shows are on twenty-four hours a day on the radio, television, and podcasts. The news has someone telling you what's happening in the world, talking 24/7. People jabber on their phones while driving, jogging, and on breaks at work.

Because we speak a lot, we often get into trouble with our words. Some of us only open our mouth to change which foot is inside it. While sometimes we put our foot in our mouth, others use words to purposefully destroy people. It's just a two-ounce slab of muscular organ, but the mouth causes many problems.

How many adults remember something painful that someone said to you as a kid? Every shark bite leaves a scar. Careless words cause pain. We must learn to control the tongue.

Throughout the Bible, warnings on the tongue pop up. James says that if you could control your tongue, you'd be mature (James 3:2), or the Greek word *teleios*, meaning "complete."[25] To say the right thing at the right time is the fruit of being a mature, complete person in Christ.

Words are like a shark's teeth. I don't want to go around with my teeth digging into people. Learning how to say the right thing at the right time is important, because we all know people who have a knack for saying the wrong thing at the wrong time. Some people bring happiness wherever they go—others *whenever* they go.

The words from your mouth now include what you type. Just because you are typing doesn't mean it's not coming from your mouth. Oftentimes, people will be inconsistent with how they talk on social media versus in real life. Social media is a large tank filled with sharks in a feeding frenzy. James 3:2 says, "If we could control our tongues, we would be perfect and could also control ourselves in every other way" (NLT).

What James is saying is that our walk with Christ all starts with the way we talk. With what we say. With what comes out of our mouth. He's saying that if you tame your tongue, everything else will follow. It's the key to growth and maturity, and it's the key to your witness for Jesus in life.

The Bible makes it clear that Christian growth and maturity are shown in how you control what comes out of your mouth. If you have a loose tongue, it shows immaturity, a lack of wisdom. If you have a tame tongue, under control, with direction and purpose, it shows Christian growth and maturity. This is a tall task without Christ.

James has quite a bit to say about our use of words. First, we'll talk about why you need to control the words that come out of your mouth. And then, we're going to look at how to do it.

Why Must I Learn to Control What I Say?

The Bible isn't focused here on times when you're hanging out with your buddies and telling jokes. Or, when you get together with your siblings or best friends and have eight conversations going at the same time. Those conversations are the spice of life. Sometimes we make fun of each other, and that's fine—unless the heart behind it is wrong. For instance, if it's sarcasm that cuts down, purposely hurting someone.

James 1:19 says, "Understand this, my dear brothers and sisters: You must all be quick to listen, slow to speak, and slow to get angry" (NLT). But, *why* must we learn to control what we say?

#1: My words steer my life.

Words set the direction of your life. James gives us a couple of illustrations. In James 3:3, he says: "We can make a large horse go wherever we want by means of a small bit in its mouth" (NLT). Even a little boy or girl can ride a two-thousand-pound horse and can direct it by putting a simple bit on the horse's tongue. The bit controls the head, which controls the whole body.

In the same way, a little bit of a word directs your life. It can either keep you on course or get you off course. And so, your words impact your direction in life.

Verse 4 continues, "A small rudder makes a huge ship

turn wherever the pilot chooses to go, even though the winds are strong" (NLT). Ships today can be several acres long. The *Knock Nevis,* a super-ship, from stern to bow is longer than the Empire State Building's height![26] Yet, that huge ship is steered by a relatively small rudder. The rudder steers the ship wherever the pilot wants it to go.

James is saying that just as a little rudder directs a ship, your tongue is the rudder directing your life. It is your steering wheel—the guidance system for your life. And, only you can control your words.

If you want to lose weight and say to yourself, "I'm never going to lose weight. I could never lose weight. I just can never do it," well, guess what? You never will. Nowhere is exactly the direction you'll go.

However, if you say you need to lose weight and you're going to make some changes to get there, regardless of the process, you just steered your mind and your body in the direction you want to head in.

For example, if you say, "I'm going to be a (teacher, construction worker, CEO, whatever you like)," then you'll go after your dream. You'll move in that direction. If you say, "I want to teach, but I don't think I could ever know enough to teach," or "I don't think I could actually build something," or "I can't succeed in business because my dad and mom were losers and I'm never going to amount to anything," you'll never fulfill your dreams.

You have a choice. If you are steering yourself in the wrong direction, that's where you're headed. It's your choice. You have your hands on the wheel and are steering somewhere with your rudder, based on the way you talk to yourself.

If you want to know where you're headed in the future, look at your conversations both with yourself and with others. Analyze your discussions with yourself: What kind of self-talk are you listening to? Are you listening to your own words as you put yourself down? Or are you being positive with yourself, encouraging yourself to be the best you can be?

We need to listen to ourselves less and instead, do more preaching to ourselves. Say it like it can be. Give yourself pep talks. What do you talk to yourself about the most? Whatever you say, you're moving in that direction. Again, as the Bible explains, your mouth steers the direction of your life. If you want to control your life, get control of your conversation and everything else will follow. It all starts with that two-ounce slab of muscular organ.

#2: My own words can destroy my life.

James adds another picture to the power of the tongue: "The tongue is a small thing, but what enormous damage it can do. A great forest can be set on fire by one tiny spark. And the tongue is a flame of fire" (James 3:5–6a TLB).

The year 2018 was California's worst fire season in history. The last one to be contained was the Woolsey fire on November 22. More than 1.8 million acres were burned.[27] You know how it started? One spark. In 2020, California has now doubled that record. You know how it started? One spark.[28]

Only you can prevent the sparks that come out of your

mouth. It's your choice. Just as a careless camper can destroy an entire national park and thousands of homes, a careless word can destroy an entire life. Many lives.

How many marriages are destroyed by careless words? How many children are scarred for life by flippant comments? How many careers are short-circuited by cruel jokes? How many relationships are devastated by painful remarks? How many nations have gone to war over boasting and mindless chatter? So many of our problems in life come by the way we talk.

Your words are like a little spark, and they can start an enormous forest fire. Have you ever met a verbal arsonist? They're always using inflammatory words. Gossip, for example, spreads faster than fire. There are verbal arsonists who go around gossiping all the time by spreading rumors—starting and spreading fires, fanning the flames instead of dousing them.

When you meet a verbal arsonist, you always have two choices. You carry two buckets with you: one bucket of gasoline and another of water. You have a choice in that moment. You will either pour gasoline on that little flame and it will explode, or pour water on it and it will be extinguished.

Gossips are always passionate, expecting you to add some fire to the spark, but you should douse it with water. For example, you might say, "That sounds important to you; you should talk to them about it." You're not their fuel, and they will come to you less and less with inflammatory commentary.

By contrast, words out of control wreak havoc and destruction. James 3:6 observes, "The tongue is set on fire by hell itself and can turn our whole lives into a blazing flame of destruction and disaster" (TLB).

The alternative to destructive words is positive words. Words under control give encouragement. They give light that points the way for people who are in the darkness. They give warmth, direction, and unity.

Your words steer the direction of your life and can damage or destroy what you have already built in your life. Your words have the power to delight or to destroy, to build up or to tear down.

Is There an Antidote to Words That Harm?

James seems to have visited a zoo when he gives us the following illustration: "All kinds of animals … have been tamed by mankind, but no human being can tame the tongue. It is a restless evil, full of deadly poison" (James 3:7–8 NIV). The tongue is restless and full of deadly poison. That's how damaging our words can be to yourself and to others.

Have you ever visited a wild animal park or drive-through safari? The lions, roaming around freely, look so tame, but signs say, "Do not get out of the car," because the animals are restless. They could strike at any moment. That's what happens with our mouths. We sometimes blurt out an offense that's full of poison. It's as dangerous as a leisurely stroll among lions, or diving into shark-infested water without a shark cage.

There's a remedy to words that hurt yourself and others. Proverbs 21:23 says, "Keep your mouth closed and you'll stay out of trouble" (TLB). Or, to invoke a cliché, a closed mouth gathers no foot. And, remember well Proverbs 13:3: "Those who control their tongue will have a long life; opening your mouth can ruin everything" (NLT).

What You Say Reveals What's in Your Heart

Your words reveal what's going on in your soul, mind, and heart. They announce to the world who you really are. Your words illustrate maturity or immaturity.

For instance, our words reveal our inconsistencies. James 3:10 says, "Out of the same mouth come praise and cursing. ... This should not be" (NIV). Pick one: goodness or evil.

When he talks about cursing here, he's not really focusing on cursing or vulgarity. He's talking about put downs, snide remarks, sarcasm, words that tear down rather than words that build up. How can you one moment say you belong to God and praise Him, and then tear someone down in the next? James is incensed. Every person is precious to God. We cannot keep praising God and tearing others down, because it's completely inconsistent. We're steering the ship this way and that, wildly sailing without direction.

Maybe you have already mastered the problem with cursing. But, maybe you haven't mastered the cutting down part.

James gets to the heart of the issue in this verse: "Can you pick olives from a fig tree, or figs from a grape vine? No, and you can't draw fresh water from a salty pool" (James 3:12 TLB). When you've got a problem with your mouth, consider the source of the problem. It's an internal problem, and it's who you are right now. The nature of the tree determines the fruit. He says that you don't grow a fig tree and hope for olives, or go to a grapevine and pick off a fig. If I've got a problem with how I talk, it's from the inside—it's an internal issue, not even a tongue issue. When you go to the well, whatever water is in the well is going to come out.

The issue is of the heart. The problem is not simply a tongue that you can't control. It's your heart.

Jesus weighed in on the issue of hearts as He walked the earth. In Matthew 12:34–35, He says, "For whatever is in your heart determines what you say. A good person produces good things from the treasury of a good heart, and an evil person produces evil things from the treasury of an evil heart" (NLT).

The mouth reveals what is really going on in the heart. Your voice is the evidence. I may kid you for a while, but eventually, my mouth will reveal what my heart is really like. It's coming from the inside. So, the heart's where the change needs to take place. Not just making a resolution like, "I'm not going to say this anymore!" That's working on the externals. You need to work on the internals.

Sometimes I hear people making excuses: "I don't know why I said that. That's not like me. I'm not like that. It just came out." Here's the reality—yes, it *is* like you. Because it welled up from the inside, the real, the natural. Not the fake. No one can be fake forever.

We've all said things we wish we could take back but can't. Even if you are sincerely sorry, you can't fix the fact you said them. Repenting is important. There's forgiveness, but it's hard to forget those words. So, understand that if you're filling your mind all the time with garbage—movies, TV shows, books, video games, whatever it might be—you're putting garbage in, so garbage is going to come out. Whatever you put into your heart is eventually going to surface.

Evidence

Here is evidence of people's true hearts. If you show me somebody with a:

- *Harsh tongue*—they have an angry heart.

- *Overactive tongue*—they have a lack of peace in their heart.

- *Judgmental tongue*—they have a guilty heart.

- *Sarcastic tongue*—they have a bitter heart.

- *Bragging tongue*—they have an insecure heart.

- *Encouraging tongue*—they have a happy heart.

- *Gentle tongue*—they have a peaceful heart.

Your words are revealing what's inside of you.

James says that whatever is on the inside is what is going to come out of the mouth. The tongue is revealing. When God helps us change, He always starts on the inside. You build a new heart. But, how do we go about creating it?

SHARK WEAK · 151

A New Heart

With issues in your life, start by admitting that you need a new heart. Confess that this is a problem for you.

A pastor had a lady in his congregation who was a terrible gossip. She knew her problem and tried to get it under control, but in her own power. One day, she admitted to him, "Pastor, the Lord has convicted me of my sin of gossip. My tongue is getting me and others into trouble."

When he guardedly asked, "Well, what do you plan to do about it?"

She replied, "I want to put my tongue on the altar."

Because she had said the same thing so many times and yet never changed, he told her, "There isn't an altar big enough."

The good news is that Jesus Christ has a big enough altar for your huge, out-of-control tongue. The solution is to get a new heart, and Jesus Christ specializes in heart transplants.

Painting the house isn't going to do any good if the foundation is cracked and crumbling. In fact, all the external things don't really matter, what you really need to start with is something more radical in terms of surgery.

You need a new heart. You need to tell Him, "God, I need You to do a supernatural miracle in my life to replace the hard, bitter, hurting, fearful, insecure, angry heart. God, I need You to work in my life and replace my heart with a heart of peace, wisdom, and encouragement."

The Bible tells us what happens when we accept what

Christ offers. Second Corinthians 5:17 says, "When someone becomes a Christian, he becomes a new person inside. He is not the same anymore. A new life has begun!" (TLB).

Christ gives you a heart transplant. It's called being born again, which means starting over. God works on the inside of you. When that happens, your tongue goes from a destroyer to a builder. It is tamed and no longer starts fires.

Once you allow Him to change your heart and then control your tongue, it's much easier to do the next step.

Listen More, Speak Less

Let's return to a verse we read earlier: "You must all be quick to listen, slow to speak, and slow to get angry" (James 1:19 NLT). If you're quick to listen and slow to speak (though we are usually the exact opposite), then you will be slow to become angry. You need to think before you speak. Two ears and one mouth means you ought to listen twice as much as you talk.

Put your mind in gear before you put your mouth in motion. Listen first.

Listening is hard to do. It takes patience. We prefer to just talk and let our point of view become known, instead of listening to others. Yet, listening is one of the greatest acts of kindness that one human can give another. It's not as easy as it sounds, and takes practice, but start listening to people—really listening.

Ask God for Help Every Day

Psalm 141:3 provides an excellent prayer to ask of God: "LORD, help me control my tongue, and help me be careful about what I say" (paraphrase). It's such a simple prayer, and God will help you—that's His promise. You must ask Him for His guidance and help.

You need God's help to break lifelong habits. Both a bit in a horse's mouth and a rudder on a ship are useless unless there's somebody in charge who knows what they're doing and how to direct. You have to make Jesus Christ the captain of your ship. Ask Him today.

What direction is your tongue steering you? Is it leading you down the pathway of conflict and bitterness? What do you talk about the most? That's the direction you're headed. What are you damaging or destroying with careless words?

When God wants to make a change, He starts on the inside. Controlling our mouth really begins with controlling our lives. You need a life leader. That's either going to be you, or it's going to be God, who knows a lot more about your life than you do. He'll make you into the person He created you to be.

And as your rudder steers you into better waters, know that sharks lurk about, waiting for you to lose your way. Keep asking for His help, and the sharks will not be able to harm you.

Chapter Seven Questions

Question: How are your words *steering* your life? Is your self-talk negative and defeatist, or hopeful and truth-based? How do you use your words (including written words on social media) to influence others—are you building up or tearing down?

_____

_____

_____

_____

_____

_____

_____

_____

_____

Question: What are some arguments that aren't worth having? When is it better to keep quiet about an issue or stay out of a debate? When should you speak out, even if it is costly? What heart attitude should you have when using your words to confront sin (Ephesians 4:15)?

Journal: Describe the most life-giving words and the most devastating words that have ever been said to you. How have others' words impacted and even directed your life? In what specific ways will you use your tongue to encourage others and help them draw closer to Christ?

_____

_____

_____

_____

_____

_____

_____

_____

_____

Action: For the next week, try an experiment with listening more and talking less. Learn about active or reflective listening—using short statements to show the speaker that you have heard them and to encourage them to tell more. Try not to share your own opinion unless the other person specifically asks. At the end of the week, evaluate: Did listening more impact your relationships? What did you learn about the people in your life?

Chapter Seven Notes

_____

_____

_____

_____

_____

_____

_____

_____

_____

_____

_____

_____

_____

_____

_____

_____

_____

_____

_____

_____

_____

_____

CONCLUSION

It's Time to Swim

Your life is surrounded by sharks that want to take bites out of you. These temptations draw you away from your true purpose, which is to glorify God by fulfilling the path He has for you. I encourage you to ask Jesus Christ to be the leader of your life, to have Him call the shots and help you with the things that are controllable—your actions. Jesus promised to give you the full life (John 10:10). Trust Him and He will show you all He created you for.

You need to remain in relationship with God. You need constant connection with Christ. The sharks that swirl around you are eager to take a nibble, get you to bleed, and start a feeding frenzy. Worry, temptation, anger, and harsh words are all ways we are pulled away from God and hurt others.

By identifying sin's bait and lures, you're less apt to leave the safety of closeness with Christ. In His protection, you can be assured of a lasting happiness that sharks cannot steal. Closeness fills your heart and mind with Him.

Yet, sometimes we bite others, eager to take them down into the depths where we swim, as we become sharks ourselves. Through our anger and our words, we use our tongues to hurt instead of help. The only way to avoid this is by staying close to Christ. Call on Him.

I pray that you do not sabotage yourself by using the wrong words. You believe what you tell yourself, because the tongue is the rudder to the ship of life. The tongue is ruled by the heart, and it's through the tongue everyone sees the status of the heart. Allow Christ to control your heart, and your tongue will speak the truth that you, and others, will follow.

Now that you know how to overcome shark bites, along with the remedy, it's time to swim. Live your life to the fullest through Him and you can be assured, you will live the best life possible. Give it all to Him daily. Who knows what adventures you will have?

About the Author

Born and raised in San Diego, Dr. Jeremy McGarity is lead pastor of Skyline Church in San Diego. Skyline is a multisite church with campuses in Lakeside, Rancho San Diego, California and Clyde, Kansas. He and his wife Janie met at Christian Heritage College (now called San Diego Christian), where Jeremy played basketball in the off-season from professional baseball with the St. Louis Cardinals, among other teams. Jeremy graduated from Christian Heritage with a degree in biblical exposition. He continued his education by earning two master's degrees from Haggard School of Theology at Azusa Pacific University: one in religion, with an emphasis in theology and ethics, and the other a Master of Divinity degree. In 2016, his love of learning led him to complete a Doctor of Ministry degree at Talbot Theological Seminary.

Jeremy is Dad to three boys and has been in full time ministry for over twenty-two years. He began as a youth pastor in South County San Diego and moved to a young adult and teaching role at High Desert Church in Victorville, California. Starting ministries, and equipping, sending, and seeing ministries grow to reach more lost people, is his passion. Jeremy loves sports, especially San Diego Padres baseball. He is enthusiastic about competing in running events including the marathon, fitness challenges, and anything else that will keep him active.

In 2007, Jeremy began building teams to start a new church, called Seven San Diego Church. On February 10, 2008, the church was launched in Otay Ranch, San Diego. The church grew to become a multisite church in 2010 with an additional location in Lakeside, East County San Diego. In 2015, after eight years of setting up and tearing down the church each Sunday in local community centers, schools, parks, and movie theaters, Seven San Diego found a church home when it adopted Living Hope Church in Lakeside. A twelve-month renovation project turned into a three-year renovation challenge, but the end result of changed lives, restored marriages, addictions broken, the lost found, and the community served has been well worth the challenges.

In November of 2018, Jeremy became the senior pastor of Skyline Church in Rancho San Diego. Seven San Diego church is now called Skyline Lakeside. We are one church in multiple locations. Our goal is to help people find and follow Jesus seven days a week.

REFERENCES

Notes

[1] "Fun Facts About Great White Sharks." Oceana. https://usa.oceana.org/fun-facts-about-great-white-sharks.

[2] Marks, Robin. "The Superlative, Sensitive Shark." *John Michael Cousteau: Ocean Adventures.* Aired July 5, 2006, on PBS. https://www.pbs.org/kqed/oceanadventures/episodes/sharks/indepth-senses.html.

[3] *Lexico,* "hubris." https://www.lexico.com/definition/hubris.

[4] Dyer, Wayne. "Your Ego Keeps You from God-Edge God Out." Posted by Edward Heffner. YouTube video, September 22, 2015. https://www.youtube.com/watch?v=WxWG8I7T5po.

[5] *Lexico,* "worry." https://www.lexico.com/en/definition/worry.

[6] *Encyclopaedia Britannica*, "middot." October 31, 2007. https://www.britannica.com/topic/middot#ref54810.

[7] LesleytheBirdNerd. "Woodpeckers Pt.1 – Why They Don't

Get Brain Damage." YouTube video, April 13, 2014. https://www.youtube.com/watch?v=Vt1mv0BJpVA.

[8] Cheney, Elizabeth. In Alonzo Bernard Webber. *Stories and Poems for Public Addresses.* George H. Doran, 1922, p. 80.

[9] Lahey, Benjamin B. "Public Health Significance of Neuroticism." *American Psychologist* 65 (2009): p. 241–256. https://www.ncbi.nlm.nih.gov/pmc/articles/PMC2792076/.

[10] Strong, James. "G3956: pas." *A Concise Dictionary of the Words in the Greek Testament and the Hebrew Bible.* Faithlife, 2019.

[11] *Lexico,* "temptation." https://www.lexico.com/en/definition/temptation.

[12] Bradberry, Travis. "How Complaining Rewires Your Brain for Negativity." TalentSmart. https://www.talentsmart.com/articles/How-Complaining-Rewires-Your-Brain-for-Negativity-2147446676-p-1.html.

[13] Bradberry, "How Complaining Rewires Your Brain."

[14] Blair, Leonardo. "Majority of Churches in Decline or Flatlining; Nearly Half See Dip in Giving, Study Says." The Christian Post. March 7, 2019. https://www.christianpost.com/news/majority-churches-decline-flatlining-nearly-half-see-dip-giving-lifeway.html.

[15] Bradberry, "How Complaining Rewires Your Brain."

[16] Marks, "The Superlative, Sensitive Shark."

[17] Edmonds, Molly. "What Causes a Shark Feeding Frenzy?" How Stuff Works. https://animals.howstuffworks.com/fish/sharks/shark-feeding-frenzy.htm.

[18] Discovery. "Great White Attacks Another Shark! | Shark Week." YouTube video, July 30, 2019. https://www.youtube.com/watch?v=UaMYSZ_i5vY.

[19] AAA. "Nearly 80 Percent of Drivers Express Significant Anger, Aggression or Road Rage." Science Daily. July 14, 2016. https://www.sciencedaily.com/releases/2016/07/160714091346.htm.

[20] Orange County Register. "Did He Check into a Roach Motel?" *The Arizona Republic.* April 25, 1995. https://www.newspapers.com/image/123417876/.

[21] Galinsky, Ellen and Judy David. *Ask the Children: The Breakthrough Study That Reveals How to Succeed at Work and Parenting.* HarperCollins, 2010.

[22] Greve, Joan E. "Who Talks More, Men Or Women? The Answer Isn't As Obvious As You Think." Time. July 16, 2014. https://time.com/2992051/women-talk-more-study/.

[23] LaRosa, John. "The $10 Billion Self-Improvement Market Adjusts to a New Generation." Market Research Blog. Marketresearch.com. October 11, 2018. https://blog.marketresearch.com/the-10-billion-self-improvement-market-adjusts-to-new-generation.

[24] Waldron, Robert. *15 Days of Prayer with Henri Nouwen.* New City Press, 2009.

[25] Strong, James. "G5406: teleios." *A Concise Dictionary of the Words in the Greek Testament and the Hebrew Bible.* Faithlife, 2019.

[26] "World's Largest Ships." Maritime Connector. http://maritime-connector.com/worlds-largest-ships/.

[27] Serna, Joseph. "2018 Was California's Worst Year of Fire Ever, Federal Report Confirms." The Los Angeles Times. March 19, 2019. latimes.com/local/lanow/la-me-ln-california-fires-record-report-20190309-story.html.

[28] Peñaloza, Marisa. "California Wildfires Near Tragic Milestone: 4 Million Acres Burned." NPR. October 2, 2020. npr.org/2020/10/02/919554698/california-wildfires-near-tragic-milestone-4-million-acres-burned.

Made in the USA
Monee, IL
18 March 2021